BRITAIN
ROME'S MOST NORTHERLY PROVINCE

BRITAIN
ROME'S MOST
NORTHERLY PROVINCE

A History of Roman Britain, A.D. 43–A.D. 450

By

G. M. DURANT

LONDON
G. BELL AND SONS, LTD

SBN 7135 1513 9

Printed in Great Britain by
The Camelot Press Ltd., London and Southampton

FOREWORD

In spite of the growing interest among young people and the general public in the visible remains of our Roman past now being dug up in almost every county in turn in Britain, the history of the Roman Occupation is still a closed book to many if not most of the inhabitants of the British Isles. Even today in many if not most schools the history of our land seems to start with '1066 and All That'. Anything before that date, both Saxon and Roman, apparently presents to many minds something intimidating in its dark obscurity, and therefore to be avoided.

This book has been written to show that study of the four centuries of the Roman Occupation need be neither intimidating nor darkly obscure. Naturally the period is not as sharply recorded (the Roman writers chiefly responsible for any record of it having only a secondary interest in Britain) as native chroniclers recorded later centuries of our history; but the main facts of the political scene are clear up to the beginning of the fifth century, and archaeology has thrown strong light upon the social life of the people, their religion and their art. In this work our aim has been to present simply and clearly all these aspects of the history of Roman Britain from A.D. 43 to about 450, and at the same time to relate the happenings of those years, where possible, to events and personalities in the wider world of the whole Roman Empire.

The book has in mind throughout the needs of those students and general readers who have not in the past been given the opportunity to learn what happened in Britain in Roman times, but who wish now that they had. Those among them who are inspired by it to know in more detail and greater depth what the Romans accomplished in this land, or who are interested in studying the conflicting theories of scholars on this debatable point or that, will find a list of more specialized works for further reading at the end.

CONTENTS

THE PLATES

I · THE CONQUEST BEGINS

It seems safe to say that nowadays practically every inhabitant of Great Britain from the age of eight upwards knows that long ago Britain was conquered by the Romans. But it is equally safe to assert that many of these would be startled and incredulous on hearing certain statements: that Britain was not conquered by Julius Caesar in 55 B.C. That the great wall from Wallsend to Solway, known as Hadrian's Wall, was not built, like the Egyptian Pyramids, by driven slaves. That the ordinary soldiers of the Roman armies in Britain were not Italians, pining under grey, rainy British skies for Mediterranean suns. That a Roman villa was only very exceptionally inhabited by a Roman. That the Romans were not brutal and tyrannous overlords, grinding the subjugated Britons beneath their heels, despising and enslaving them, denying them freedom and every privilege. That during the four centuries of the Occupation the land was not one vast military camp, with soldiers swarming everywhere.

The truth is that after 55 and 54 B.C. Julius Caesar had other things to do, more important in his estimation, than troubling about an island on the extreme northern rim of the Roman Empire. Hadrian's Wall was built entirely by legionary soldiers. The men of the Roman army were recruited from all the provinces of the Roman Empire, and might be Britons, Dacians, Gauls, Tungrians, Dalmatians, Thracians, Spaniards and a host of others, speaking all manner of languages and worshipping all kinds of native gods. Roman villas are correctly so called only because they were built to a Roman plan, with Roman help, and it was normally wealthy romanized Britons who lived in them. And it was part of Roman policy to win over those conquered to the acceptance of the superior Roman civilization; to give them a share in its benefits and a stake in the Empire —even, in lesser matters, a measure of self-government.

It has often been pointed out that the period of the Roman occupation of Britain—from A.D. 43 to some date between 407 and 428, or perhaps even a few years later than that—is almost as long as the stretch of years from the times of Shakespeare and Queen Elizabeth I to the present day. Between Queen Elizabeth I's day and ours many changes have taken place. Many changes likewise took place during the four centuries of the Roman occupation. People were not living in exactly the same conditions in A.D. 360 as they had been in 60.   Great changes occurred especially in the army during those years, and in the organization of the province of Britain, reflecting changes in the organization of the Empire itself.   *Tempora mutantur*, as the Romans used to say. Nothing stands still while the centuries glide by.   Changing fashions in dress are but one trivial aspect of the ever changing modes of life.   'The old order changeth, yielding place to new'—though whether the new is inevitably better than the old is a debatable point.   In the case of the Roman Empire it was not.   And so in the end the Roman Empire passed away, leaving only the memory of its greatness behind, the abiding recollection of the *immensa Romanae pacis maiestas*—the measureless majesty of the Roman Peace.

So let us come to the truth of the matter.   Julius Caesar, ✳ as we have said, had other things to think about after 54 B.C.   First, the dangerous revolt of the lately subdued tribes of Gaul under their heroic leader, Vercingetorix, and then his desire to grasp supreme power in Rome which led to civil war between him and Pompey.   It is doubtful if he ever meant his two descents upon Britain to be much more than reconnaissances in force, similar to his crossing of the Rhine (over that bridge with whose construction so many of us have struggled in the *De Bello Gallico*) to terrorize the marauding Germans by giving them a taste of Roman might. He advanced in Britain in 54 beyond the Thames, won a battle against the native chieftain Cassivellaunus, and then departed after demanding hostages and levying tribute. The payment of the tribute seems soon to have ceased, and Caesar never came to Britain again.   Ten years after his second visit he was assassinated.   Thereafter, for nearly a century, Britain was left undisturbed.

But the Romans had tidy minds, as their language would prove if nothing else did. Apart from the fact that it was supposed that there were riches of gold, wool and corn to be had in Britain, it distressed many of them to think that there should be an island independent of Rome so near the Roman domains in Gaul, a ravelled edge, as it were, of the close-knit cloak of the Empire. Even Roman writers said that something ought to be done about it. We perhaps remember Horace's

> . . . Praesens divus habebitur
> Augustus adiectis Britannis
> imperio gravibusque Persis[1]

'. . . then shall Augustus be held divine when Britons and dread Persians shall be added to the empire'; and when at last there came an emperor not so busy as his predecessors had been, and when there were legions to spare for the enterprise, something actually was done. In A.D. 43 Claudius decided that the time had come to knit up the ravelled edge into the Roman Empire and bring *Britannia ultima Orbis*—Britain at the edge of the world—under Roman rule.

Claudius is not one of the more spectacular Roman emperors. He suffered from some defect in his speech, he halted on one leg and had trembling hands. In his unhappy youth he had tended to be the laughing-stock of those around him, the butt of their practical jokes. So not unnaturally he had withdrawn as far as possible from society and had devoted himself to study, especially the study of Roman history and antiquities. He became learned, and like the stage scholar and don, absent-minded; but a few had realized that he was by no means such a fool as he looked. He was about fifty when he became emperor. Two years later he decided to embark upon the enterprise which the great Augustus had considered too difficult to attempt, and the grim Tiberius had shrunk from: the conquest of Britain.

If this was rushing in where angels feared to tread his temerity was justified by his success. He chose the elderly general Aulus Plautius, and the Second, Ninth, Fourteenth and Twentieth Legions to carry out the task. We may

[1] *Odes*, III. v.

smile at the arrangement he made with Aulus Plautius.
Claudius was not without the characteristic imperial vanity.
The general was to clear away initial opposition, advance as
far as seemed desirable, and then, when the decisive battle
would appear to be looming ahead, he was to send for the
emperor, who would cross to Britain and win the final
victory.

Aulus Plautius landed with his legions on what was then
a tiny island off the island of Thanet, in Kent—Richborough; in Latin, Rutupiae. (There have been geographical changes in these parts since those far-off days.
Thanet, whereon stand Ramsgate and Margate today,
Herne Bay and suchlike resorts, is no longer an island,
though it is still called one, and you approach Richborough
dry-shod along a semi-rural lane from Sandwich.) Here at
Richborough Aulus Plautius established his camp, the
earthworks of which are still plainly visible inside the later
fort which we shall have occasion to mention much later.
What resistance, if any, he encountered is not clear, but anyhow, it was not enough to deter him. The natives, it would
seem, had withdrawn into the Weald (that is, the Wild or
Wold land, uncultivated forest and scrub) and apparently
did little more than harass the Romans' foragers.

It is difficult for us now, used as we have become to the
roar of traffic on our motorways, the industrialization of
once rural areas, the ugly pylons striding from hill to hill, the
atomic stations on formerly remote estuaries, and the ubiquitous houses spreading rapidly in our over-populated
island, to imagine Britain as it was in the days when Aulus
Plautius's legions first looked upon it and marched through
it. The unchanging ramparts of the Welsh mountains, the
uncultivatable, wild Yorkshire moors, the inhospitable
pinnacles of rock off the Cornish coast remain as they ever
were, but the southern Weald, the Midland plains and the
gentler hills and valleys would now be unrecognizable to
those legionaries of nineteen hundred years ago, as they
would be to the Britons who then sparsely inhabited them.

The only roads were primitive tracks, impassable in winter,
trodden out by those who journeyed from one place to
another. Forests, dark and impenetrable, wolf-haunted

and dangerous with wild boars, covered two-thirds of the land. Vast areas round Romney and Glastonbury, Thorney and Crowland were swampy marshes, and the fens of East Anglia were stretches of shining mere sprinkled with reedy islands where half uncouth British fowlers and fishers, seeking a precarious existence, paddled their skin canoes under illimitable skies. And standing up against the driving clouds on the hilltops were the strongholds of the tribal chieftains: we can still see their impressive earthworks at Wolstonebury and Cissbury on the South Downs, at Eggardon and above all Maiden Castle in Dorset, or in the north, on Ingleborough. Below these there would cluster the beehive-shaped, thatched huts—some, for the sake of warmth, dug bowl-like into the ground—of the peasants, who would, at the approach of danger, take refuge with their flocks and herds behind the defences of their chieftain's stronghold on the hills above. Indeed, some of these hill-top enclosures seem to have been little more than corrals. These strongholds, with their associated huts below, Caesar in his *Commentaries* called *oppida*— 'towns', for lack of a better Latin word to describe what did not exist among the Romans; but towns in the Roman and modern sense there were none in pre-Roman Britain. Even the 'capitals' of tribal kings, like the Wheathampstead of Cassivellaunus or the Colchester of Cunobelinus, were merely larger strong-holds with perhaps a thicker concentration of peasants' huts outside their stockades. Such Celtic *oppida*, often of great extent, situated not on hill-tops but in flat country, though less spectacular than the hill-top strongholds, would in A.D. 43 have been defended by their proximity to vast forests or far stretching marshland, or by natural waters or dykes which were dug to encircle them.

Owing to the lack of adequate communications as well as to the extent of dense forest, these native *oppida* tended to be isolated communities. One tribe might consider even its near neighbours as foreigners. Their lack of cohesion made them immediately vulnerable to well organized foes like the Roman legionaries. Their frantic courage and warlike zeal were no efficient substitutes for the will and power to com-bine against a common enemy. But they were not savages, clad in bearskins; hairy, yelling barbarians capering before astonished invaders. We have Caesar's authority for stating that the inhabitants of the south-eastern parts of Britain, through which Aulus Plautius now proceeded to advance, definitely had some civilization. For many years these Britons—the Cantiaci of Kent—had been in close contact with the Gauls of northern France, Celts like themselves; and in the years between the defeat of Vercingetorix by Caesar and the coming of Aulus Plautius to Britain these Gauls had become completely romanized, and had passed on a tincture of their romanization to the Britons who had intercourse with them—principally through trade. Some of the British chieftains were civilized and romanized enough to mint money. Not long ago a schoolboy of Folkestone, on the Kent coast, found in the hills behind that town a silver coin which proved to have been minted by a chieftain or petty prince called Amminus.

This Amminus is otherwise unknown. A more illustrious British leader who also minted money, gold as well as silver and copper imitating Roman coinage, was Cunobelinus of the Catuvellauni—or Cymbeline, as Shakespeare more harmoniously calls. him. Cymbeline reigned a very long time over the Catuvellauni, and as high king of Britain—the Roman historians refer to him as *rex Brittonum*, though his power certainly did not extend over the whole of Britain— held sway over Kent. Consequently it was his two sons, Togodumnus and Caratacus, ruling jointly over their father's lands after his death, two years before Aulus Plautius's appearance in Thanet, who met the invading legions and led the resistance to them. This stiffened and at last became formidable as the Roman general reached the river Medway where it begins to broaden to its estuary in the neighbour-hood of the present city of Rochester.

The cathedral which now looks out upon the Medway at Rochester, the ruins of the Norman castle, the cement works in the valley, the houses immortalized by Dickens, the vessels passing up and down these tidal reaches, we must think away if we are to imagine that first encounter of Britons and Romans in the conquest of Britain. There were no build-ings of any size there then, if any buildings at all; only a

wide sheet of water at high tide, and as the tide went out a
stretch of riverine mud, difficult to traverse.   In the distance,
in those days, rose the wooded hills of north Kent, with only
a few beehive-shaped, thatched huts scattered here and
there over the valley below them.   It was the river, of course,
that had checked Aulus Plautius's advance, for if there had
been any bridge over it the Britons had taken care to destroy
it; and here it was, at this obstacle to his progress, that the
two sons of Cymbeline had chosen to resist him.

The ensuing battle was long and stubborn, but the British
forces gave way at last, fleeing away into the hills and making
off in a north-westerly direction to the next defensible
position, the valley of the Thames.   Aulus Plautius steadily
pursued them, and came up with them at a place not
mentioned by name, but which was probably a little Celtic
trading-station on the tidal reaches of the river, to become
famous afterwards as Londinium (London).

This was another marshy spot, though no doubt more
inhabited, with traders' huts on the banks of the river and a
bridge, doubtless of timber struts and planks, over the
water, very likely on the site of the mediaeval London Bridge
and not far from where the modern one spans the water.
Here too there were wooded heights looking down on the
valley, and low hills just over the river with tributary streams
flowing in the hollows between them.   It was in this place,
in an engagement similar to the one at the Medway crossing,
that Aulus Plautius won his second victory; and here that
Togodumnus was probably killed, though the possibility
exists that he fell in the battle at the Medway.   In any event
he perished, and Caratacus was left to lead the resistance to
the invaders alone.

Aulus Plautius's objective was now Caratacus's capital,
some fifty miles off to the north-east: Colchester in Essex, or
as the Romans were to call it, Camulodunum. But since the
capture of this chief stronghold of the leader of the resistance
would be a decisive victory the old general thought the time
had come to invite the emperor over, so that this final
victory might seem to be his. Claudius came with an
imperial train, and with elephants, like another Hannibal;
though what use he thought these beasts would be is not

clear. What was more to the point, he brought reserves, and landing no doubt at Rutupiae, which was destined to become the foremost port of entry into Britain throughout the Roman period, he made his way to where Aulus Plautius was dutifully awaiting him, and on they marched together.

The undaunted Caratacus made one more bid to save his capital and his dominions, but all his valour was in vain. He was forced to flee to terrain more suited to the warfare he was determined to wage upon the Romans—the wild mountains and desolate passes of Wales, where also he could count upon the help of the Silures of the south, and the Ordovices of the north of that country in his stand. His personal followers fled westward with him; but all the tribes of south-eastern Britain—of what we now call East Anglia, Kent, Surrey and Sussex—submitted to the invaders. A king of the Iceni—Prasutagus, of whom we shall speak again—and another of the Regnenses of Sussex—Cogidubnus—had so subserviently hastened to make their submission to the conquerors that they received, as they had hoped, the best terms. Their states were made vassal states, and they were allowed to remain as vassal kings in them. They gained the title of 'allies of the Roman people'—Tacitus refers to Cogidubnus of the Regnenses as 'our most faithful ally'. To this day in Chichester (Noviomagus Regnensium, the capital of Cogidubnus)[1] you may see preserved under the portico of the Council House an inscribed tablet from a vanished building which the king set up round about this time in this neighbourhood, using the Latin language for his inscription:

> To Neptune and Minerva, this temple is dedicated for the welfare of the divine house by the authority of Tiberius Claudius Cogidubnus, king and legate of Augustus in Britain . . .

from which it is obvious that the former British chieftain had not only adopted or been granted Latin names but was very proud of them and of his standing with the Romans.

---

[1] It is possible that a Roman villa, or palace, of immense size, still being excavated at Fishbourne on the outskirts of Chichester, Sussex, may have been built for himself by this king, to live in in Roman style and luxury, from rewards given him by the Romans for his adherence to their cause.

Although the island was less than half conquered Britain was formally constituted a province of the Roman Empire, with Camulodunum as the seat of the governor and the procurator—the former the military commander, the latter, independent of him and recognizing the authority of the emperor alone, a Treasury official. And as a perpetual reminder and symbol of the mighty and eternal power of Rome, made manifest in the representative of the mysterious and divine force that upheld the Roman city and people, namely, the emperor himself, a great temple was built in Camulodunum, named, after his death in A.D. 54, the temple of Divus Claudius.

II · RESISTANCE

After sixteen days in Britain Claudius departed to enjoy a triumph in Rome, and Aulus Plautius was left in command in the island to deal with those tribes which had not yet been subdued.

We should remember that our knowledge of these events comes from Roman authors. In the first place, these had not as great an interest in Britain as we have, and consequently they often omit from their accounts details which we would find interesting; in the second place, much of their writings has in centuries gone by been lost, so that we discover gaps in the early history of our land which we are able to bridge only with guesswork. Thus we have no distinct and minute account of exactly what Aulus Plautius did in the four years he stayed in Britain. It would seem, as far as we can judge, that he organized his troops in three divisions. The Ninth Legion he sent northwards, through Cambridgeshire and round the edge of the Fens, and it established its base camp at Ratae (Leicester). The Fourteenth and Twentieth Legions went north-westerly through the Midlands to some shadowy base unknown on the way to Wales. The third division, however, which was sent south-westerly, we know more about.

It was composed of the Second Legion, and commanded by a general named Vespasian, a homely Sabine peasant, unhandsome and unimaginative, but a rock of determination and common sense, who later became Emperor; the incidents of his life, including his doings in Britain, are consequently well recorded.

The Roman writer Suetonius says that 'he fought thirteen battles with the natives and added to the Roman Empire two powerful tribes, twenty towns [*oppida*] and Vectis Insula' (the Isle of Wight). The two tribes were the Belgae, the inhabitants of the land between the Solent and Somerset; and the Durotriges, who lived in Dorset. The 'towns' were,

of course, the Celtic hill-fortresses which we have mentioned
before. One of the thirteen was undoubtedly Maiden
Castle, that immense, brooding earthwork two miles from
Dorchester, which is still plainly visible. As one walks towards its eastern flank today, along the road from Dorchester,
and sees it ahead lying up against the sky—particularly if
storm-clouds are welling up over it—it looks like some
crouching monster of prehistoric days petrified in sombre
and majestic menace.

The interior of this great Iron Age stronghold was
excavated by Sir Mortimer Wheeler in 1934. He found
abundant evidence there that at its east gate the native
defenders had made a last valiant but desperate stand against
Vespasian's legionaries. Behind them were their cattle and
other possessions, their wives and children, sheltering within
the massive earthen ramparts, which would then have been
crowned with a timber palisade; these they were determined
to guard to their last gasp. A barrage of ballista arrows
from the legionary artillery was followed by the advance of
the infantry, hacking its way upwards from one earthen
rampart to the next. The Romans set fire to some of the
circular huts near the innermost earth-bank before the
entrance, and under cover of the clouds of smoke from the
flames they stormed the gate. The stubbornness of the
British resistance had infuriated the soldiers, and they showed
no restraint as they cut down men and women, young and
old alike. It was the bones of all these fallen, with pathetic
offerings of beakers and food-vessels laid by the survivors
beside them, that the excavators found at and about the east
gate; and among them were the remains of a British defender
who had evidently, in the early stages of the attack, caught a
Roman ballista arrow in his spine. There it is, nineteen
hundred years after, still lying in his broken backbone. You
may see it today in the Dorchester Museum.

This is the kind of scene that lies behind Suetonius's
laconic statement that Vespasian took 'thirteen *oppida*'.
Twenty or thirty years after the Romans induced the
remnant of the inhabitants of Maiden Castle to move down
from the hill and make their homes where Dorchester now
stands. But in A.D. 43 Vespasian, disregarding this remnant,

pressed on westwards, establishing his base, as far as we can
judge, somewhere round about where Gloucester now stands.

Aulus Plautius remained four years in Britain.   In those
four years all the southernmost parts of the island below a
line drawn approximately from Bath in Somerset, through
Silchester in Hampshire to London near the mouth of the
Thames, with a loop northwards to take in Colchester in
Essex, had been subdued.   His successor, Ostorius Scapula,
pushed this line out farther.   The legion which had been
based on Ratae (Leicester) he moved forward to Lindum
Colonia (Lincoln); the Second Legion in the neighbourhood
of Gloucester was brought further west to Isca (Caerleon), on
the borders of south Wales; while the Twentieth and
Fourteenth Legions which had advanced through the
Midlands worked their way on to Viroconium (Wroxeter),
almost equally near to the borders of North Wales.

To Ostorius Scapula also belongs the distinction of found-
ing the first Roman city (in our sense of the word, as well as
his) in Britain—at Caratacus's old capital, now the centre of
the administration of the province, Camulodunum (Colchester).   It was also the first 'colony' in Britain—that is to
say, a town built primarily for, and mostly inhabited by, at
any rate at this early period, time-expired (retired) Roman
soldiers called *veterani*, who were granted allotments of land
and expected to keep an eye on any possible hostile movements of the natives round about them.   Another important
part of their duties was to be a centre of Roman influence
which would permeate the neighbourhood in time and by
degrees romanize the inhabitants of it.   The foundation of
'colonies' in the midst of newly conquered peoples had been
a part of Roman policy from earliest times, but this was the
first example of it in Britain.   In the case of Camulodunum
Ostorius Scapula evidently thought too that the veterans
would act as a garrison in the eastern parts of Britain while
the only legions he had at his disposal were engaged in
combating trouble in the north and west.

For the mountains of Wales, among which the warlike
Ordovices and Silures lived, and the wild regions of the
north, from Derbyshire to the Solway Firth, the home of the
untamed Brigantes, were an ever-present menace to the new

province. As soon as the conquest of the southerly part of
Britain was more or less accomplished these fierce, restless
tribes began their marauding inroads into what was now
Roman territory. Wales was a particular thorn in the flesh
of the governor, because it had not only kindly received
Caratacus, the exiled son of Cymbeline, who had fled westwards, we remember, after the Roman capture of Camulodunum, but had given him military command, and it was he
who was now leading them against the Romans. For three
years Caratacus captained the Silures of South Wales in a
series of campaigns against the Romans, and their base at
Isca (Caerleon); but as soon as Ostorius Scapula concen-
trated his efforts upon them Caratacus withdrew to the
Ordovices in North Wales. The governor, apparently
thinking that if only he could either capture or kill Caratacus
Welsh resistance would crumple up, left the south and
followed him; and after many trials came upon him strongly
entrenched among precipitous mountains—the spot is not
now identifiable.

It is said that before the ensuing battle Caratacus played a
defiant and heroic part most inspiring to his Celtic confederates. In one of the speeches Roman historians conventionally put into the mouths of generals addressing their
troops before battle he reminded them of the Britons who
had inhabited his kingdom a hundred years ago, and how they
had turned back the all-conquering Julius Caesar; he
described to them what the Roman yoke would mean to men
who had always been free, and vehemently urged them to
save themselves and their families from tribute, slavery and
dishonour. Thereupon, roused by such memories and such
exhortations, the warriors of both Ordovices and Silures
swore by their tribal gods that they would either conquer the
invading foe or die.

Nevertheless, in spite of the Britons' determined stand, it
was the Romans who, though with heavy loss, won this, the
last battle that Caratacus was destined to fight. He had
rallied his forces after the initial Roman breakthrough, and
had fought stubbornly till his line was broken for the second
time and his adherents, desperate at last, fled in all directions.
Caratacus himself, still unconquered in spirit, escaped to the

Brigantes, hoping to encourage that fierce and militant tribe to join him in repelling the foe—or at least in wearing the Romans down by continuous harassment. This he might have achieved, had not the queen of the tribe, Cartimandua, been pro-Roman—whether by inclination or from policy we do not know. She seized the exiled king of the Catuvellauni and handed him over, with his family, to the Roman governor. Ostorius Scapula sent him to Rome for Claudius to decide on his fate.

Caratacus seems to have conducted himself in the presence of the emperor with such dignity and courage that the not unkindly Claudius was impressed, and ordered his life to be spared and him and his family to be freed. A well-known anecdote detailed by one of the Roman writers, Dio Cassius, relates how, as the former Catuvellaunian king looked round upon the luxurious and highly civilized houses which met his astonished gaze in Rome, he observed, 'And yet the owners of these must needs covet our poor huts in Britain.' To those huts he of course never returned. He seems to have been granted some sort of pension, and to have died in honourable captivity in Italy.

This end of a gallant British warrior king may please the tender-hearted; it will probably disappoint those who like their heroes to perish fighting to the death in a dramatic blaze of glory.

III · THE REVOLT OF BOUDICCA AND THE ICENI

Ostorius Scapula was mistaken if he thought that the resistance of the Welsh to Roman conquest would fade away with the disappearance of Caratacus from their midst. For nine years, from A.D. 50 to 59, their war-like struggles against the forces of succeeding governors continued. Nor was any further progress made against the northern tribes, the Brigantes. In the year 59, however, there came to Britain a very determined, ruthless and inflexible governor, who was also a general of considerable skill: Suetonius Paulinus. We are not sure whether he or one of his predecessors moved the Twentieth Legion from its station at Viroconium nearer to North Wales at Deva (Chester). Here the Twentieth was destined to stay for nearly the whole period of the Occupation, watching North Wales while the Second watched the southern Silures from Isca—where it also was destined to stay till the fourth century. Meanwhile the Ninth remained for the time being at Lindum Colonia (Lincoln is a later abbreviation of the Latin name).

Suetonius Paulinus, on his arrival as governor—which involved holding the chief military command—had a definite objective. He was determined to exterminate the Druids. These were the ancient native priests—though they had nothing whatever to do with Stonehenge, which was built as a temple, presumably to the Sun, a thousand years or more before the Druids were thought of. The Druids never built temples. Their recondite ceremonies took place in the green and gloomy depths of the vast oak forests of those days; though what these ceremonies were, except that they demanded the sacrifice of both animals and human beings, we do not know, since the Druids' teachings were not committed to writing, but were handed down by word of mouth and held only in mortal memories. We know also that these white-robed priests performed some mystic rite connected with the mistletoe—the 'Golden Bough' of Antiquity, which Aeneas of Virgil's *Aeneid* had to find to gain access to the Underworld; the plant which northern myths tell us killed the beloved and beautiful god Baldur. The Druid priests cut it from oak-trees with a golden sickle, and they chanted their oracular messages to the people while in a state of trance, resembling that of the prophetess of Delphi at the navel of the world.

They had spells and charms, and wielded such power and authority over the people, who reverenced them for their unfathomable knowledge of the sacred mysteries, that they were easily the leaders of any opposition to a foe, especially as they were chosen from among the warriors of the tribes. It was not their religion that the Romans, tolerant in such matters, objected to—apart from its demand for human sacrifice; it was this power they exercised over the people of inspiring them to revolt in which they became the leaders. One of their greatest strongholds was the island of Anglesey, known to the Romans as Mona; and against this island Suetonius Paulinus now prepared to advance.

His preparations took a year to complete, for he had to build ships on the Dee to ferry his infantry across from the mainland; the cavalry were to swim the Menai Strait at low tide. When the boats were ready he advanced from Deva into North Wales, probably to a spot near Bangor. He met no opposition, for all the Ordovices were assembled on Mona to defend their ancient forest sanctuaries.

A dramatic scene met the Romans' eyes as they came near to Mona. A line of warriors stood thick as flies along the island shore; among them were women dressed in black, rushing about so that the legionaries must have been reminded of the implacable Furies of Greek legend; their wild, unbound hair streamed behind them, they held blazing torches in their hands. In the rear were the weird, white-robed Druid priests, making fiery sacrifice to their gods; their arms were raised to heaven as they called down curses upon the invaders.

At this unwonted and chilling sight even the Roman legionaries paused in dismay. It needed the encouragement of their officers to drive them on, as they demanded why they should fear a rabble of frenzied women and fanatical priests. But at last the Romans charged, and broke the warrior line. No quarter was asked or given. The legionaries drove the foe back upon the fires of their own sacrifices, and those who were not consumed in the flames they massacred, warriors, women and priests indiscriminately. And when the slaughter was over the soldiers hacked and hewed among the trees, and brought the sacred groves crashing to the ground.

Then came a dramatic climax to the scene, as if the prayers of the Druids to their gods had in the moment of their extermination been heard and answered. News was brought post-haste to Suetonius Paulinus that all eastern Britain, quiet for the last ten years, was ablaze with revolt.

This was the year A.D. 61. The revolt was led by Boudicca, queen of the Iceni—the people of present-day Norfolk and Suffolk—and she was carrying all before her as she advanced towards Camulodunum, seat and symbol of the Roman government. What was it that had happened to cause such a revolt in the hitherto untroublesome plain-land of Britain?

Prasutagus, the husband of Boudicca, was, as we have said above, the other king who, with Cogidubnus of the Reg-nenses, had early submitted to the Romans, and like him had been allowed to keep his kingdom as a vassal state. But when he died in 61 without male heirs, it was found that he—thinking to forestall trouble, no doubt—had left half his kingdom and possessions to the Roman Empire. Officials were thereupon sent by the procurator to effect the transfer; and they had been guilty of gross misconduct in the business. They were typical of the Roman official at his worst—and at his worst the Roman official could be very bad indeed. Rapacious and ruffianly, they had seized not half, but the whole of the kingdom, and in doing so devastated the palace, stripped some of the richest of the Iceni of their estates, arrested the late king's widow, Boudicca, and when she opposed their doings scourged her and outraged her two young daughters.

When they heard this the Iceni rose as one man to avenge their queen's wrongs, and the injuries inflicted upon their chief men. They were immediately joined by the neighbouring tribe of the Trinovantes, who had their own grievances, and were equally resentful of the doings of the Romans. We mentioned before that Camulodunum had been established a 'colony', and its inhabitants were mostly *veterani* from the army, granted allotments of land by way of pension on retirement. These allotments had to come from somewhere; so land was taken from the natives to supply them. Consequently, when the revolt against Roman rule broke out the Trinovantes immediately leapt to arms.

Queen Boudicca placed herself at the head of all those who rose to redress her wrongs. From all accounts she seems to have been a woman of resolute character and forceful personality. She sprang from illustrious British ancestors, and the signs of her aristocratic lineage were amply shown in her bearing. Tall, and of regal dignity, she stood erect in her war-chariot, enveloped, so they say, in a long mantle girt with a gold belt; her unbound golden hair floated to the ground. Apparently even tough warriors obeyed her when she commanded. It is a pity we have no likeness left us of this queen who stands with the exiled king Caratacus as a defiant and undaunted champion of liberty against tyranny, the rights of men against oppression—for of course the modern London statue of her in her chariot is a fanciful portrait; nevertheless, in the few remarks about her appearance made by contemporary writers we can see the vague but dominating outline of the queen.

The first objective of the combined forces of the Iceni and Trinovantes was Camulodunum, the monument of Roman triumph and the stronghold of Roman tyranny. The Roman wall which we can nowadays trace round Colchester for almost its entire circuit did not then exist. It was built afterwards, in case any such disaster ever came again like the one that befell the town in the terrible year 61. Camulodunum then had no wall, no ditch, no defence works whatever; no fort, no place that could be defended except the massive stone-built temple of Divus Claudius. The meagre Roman force of two hundred men sent by the frightened procurator crowded into this, but the place was besieged and soon stormed. Straightway it was razed to the ground by the exulting insurgents, for to them it was a symbol—as it had been meant to be—of the eternal power of Rome made manifest in the deified emperor to whom it had been dedicated. The Trinovantes, moreover, had an extra grudge against it, for it was they who had had to pay exorbitantly for the upkeep of its priests and sacrifices. They left nothing of it standing above ground. Only the massive foundations, which they could not destroy, remained. They remain to this day, underneath the Norman castle built a thousand years after Boudicca's revolt; and in the Second World War the inhabitants of modern Colchester used them as an air-raid shelter.[1]

After the storming of the temple everyone, women as well as men, who had ever been friendly to the Romans, the enraged and victorious Britons killed (so the Roman writers say) with savage tortures. Then they turned to confront the one Roman legion—the Ninth—which had been left by Paulinus in the eastern parts of Britain, at Lindum Colonia. It was commanded by Petillius Cerealis, who now hastened to the rescue. But the Britons cut the legionary infantry to pieces. Cerealis managed to escape with only some of the cavalry.

At this resounding victory all the native tribes in the vicinity surged forward to swell Boudicca's army. The procurator, terrified when he considered his part in bringing on this catastrophe, took to his heels and sought safety in Gaul; and with the governor far off in Wales, and no military protection now left them, the Romans and their British adherents—for there were many Britons friendly to the Romans, even thus early—fled to the only two towns in eastern Britain which seemed to offer any refuge—Verulamium (St. Albans) and Londinium. This was the situation which had been reached when reports of the revolt came to Suetonius as the massacre of the Druids was ending and the destruction of their sacred groves was completed.

He at once gathered all the forces that were available—the Twentieth and Fourteenth Legions—and sent orders to the commander of the Second at Isca to join him. These

---

[1] Presumably the temple was afterwards rebuilt, for the Romans would hardly have allowed this memorial of their defeat to remain; but if so we have no mention of it.

orders were never obeyed, the commander of the Second
being apparently panic-stricken. Paulinus hastened right
across Britain to the old Celtic trading-station of Londinium,
here mentioned specifically by that name in Roman writings
for the first time. He was so alarmed by the situation when
he reached Londinium, which also was an unwalled, indefensible town, that he decided to fall back upon the only
parts of Britain now left in Roman hands—the neighbour-
hoods of Deva and Isca on the borders of Wales. He proclaimed to the crowds in Londinium that any of them who
cared to journey under his protection could do so, and many
panic-stricken refugees, men, women and children, old and
young, followed him as he withdrew, trailing pitiably on the
flanks or in the rear of the legions. The few who stayed
behind were massacred by Boudicca's tribal hordes when
they came storming on from the slaughter of the refugees at
Verulamium and the fiery destruction of that town also, and
burst, unopposed and triumphant, into the Roman paved
streets of London—which then occupied hardly as extensive
an area as the 'City' properly so called today. Soon, a
funeral pyre for the slaughtered, Londinium, like Camulodunum and Verulamium, was flaming red to the sky.

How long ago all this seems now—so long, that it is almost
impossible to believe that it ever happened. But those who,
in modern times, have for various reasons dug deeply below
London's soil have come upon a thick layer of ashes: the
ashes of the fires Boudicca's followers lit, the visible remains
of the holocaust of her fearful coming nineteen hundred
years ago. Then the dead years quicken again, and the
past, stirring and rising, lays its fingers upon present time.

The Roman writers probably exaggerated when they
stated that 70,000 Romans and pro-Roman Britons and
traders from Gaul perished in these atrocious massacres, but
undoubtedly the numbers of her hated enemies slain by
Boudicca must have been very large.

Suetonius found his retreat westward seriously hampered
by the vast crowd of refugees straggling along, more often
behind than with his legionaries. At last, when he reached a
place where his wings and rear were covered by forest, so
that he could not be outflanked by the superior numbers of

the enemy, now close behind him, he made the bold resolve
to turn and face the exultant queen and her frenzied hordes,
even without the Second Legion, which had still not joined
him, though it is probable that by this time the governor had
received reinforcements from other quarters.   Boudicca was
so drunk with success that she did not stop to think out the
best way of opposing her wild and madly enthusiastic forces
to the cool, calculating strategy of the Roman commander
of a trained and disciplined army.   She had probably never
heard how Julius Caesar used to say that only the first rush
of a Celtic army was to be dreaded.   But Suetonius, who no
doubt *had* heard, soon found out how true that saying was.
The Romans, advancing in ordered array, the legionary
infantry in a dense column in the centre, the auxiliaries on
each side of it, the cavalry on the flanks, having first with-
stood the rush of the foe, next pierced the centre of the
opposing army.   Immediately many fled; those who tried
to hold their ground were pushed back to ultimate confusion among their wagons and miscellaneous camp equip-
ment in the midst of the trees in their rear, where their
women and children were congregated, eager to see the
victory, which by now they assumed to be certain, of the
British forces.   It was then the Romans' turn to massacre
without quarter.   Boudicca escaped from the mêlée, but to
prevent herself being captured by the Romans and paraded
in chains in a Roman triumph, she committed suicide by
poisoning herself.

Where this final battle between Boudicca and Suetonius
took place we do not know, any more than we know where
Caratacus met his last defeat.   But we do know that in the
succeeding months Suetonius ravaged the lands of the rebels,
slaughtering and laying waste with fearful thoroughness and
bringing desolation wherever he went, especially among the
Iceni.   It was, perhaps, the new procurator, Julius Classicianus, who, seeing that more conciliatory methods were
likely to bring peace nearer than ever the governor's
merciless punishment of the rebels would, caused reports of
Suetonius's doings to be brought to the notice of the then
emperor, Nero.   But whoever their author may have been,
the reports reached Nero, who recalled Suetonius Paulinus,

and appointed a milder man governor of Britain in his stead. The more moderate measures of this governor, and the wiser councils of Julius Classicianus, had their effect. Presently all trouble died in the south and east of Britain; discontent passed away; even thus early some of the advantages of Roman civilization began to be apparent to the Britons of these parts. The procurator who had helped to bring about peace, Julius Classicianus, died, presumably in office, in London; his tombstone has been found, broken in two and much damaged, and can now be seen in the British Museum.

IV · ROMAN ROADS

The next ten years saw the first steps towards romanization of the southern and eastern parts of Britain,
which, after the suppression of Boudicca's revolt, never
gave further trouble to the conquerors. The towns that
Boudicca had destroyed were speedily rebuilt, and soon
recovered, and even increased, their former prosperity.
And though Camulodunum continued for a while as the seat
of the administration of the province, there seems already
to have been a realization that the old Celtic trading station
of Londinium was really the natural geographical nerve-
centre of the province, for when the Romans turned their
attention to communications it was Londinium that they
made the starting-point of most of their main highways.

Good roads were one of the greatest gifts of the conquerors
to the lands they conquered. They facilitated trade and
travel and brought prosperity to the towns to which they
gave birth; they made intercourse between them possible
and so gave rise to a sense of unity over large areas that had
not existed before. But first and foremost, in Britain as it
had been elsewhere in the Empire, the making of good roads
was a necessity of conquest. We realize this when we notice
that the three earliest main roads that the Romans laid down
run from London north-west to Viroconium (Wroxeter),
north to Lindum Colonia (Lincoln) and west by Calleva
(Silchester) to Isca Dumnoniorum (Exeter). It was along
these roads that the three conquering columns of the invading
army went from Londinium—from Londinium, not Camulodunum, the capital—to the conquest of the south-west, the
Midlands and the north, and Londinium must have served
as the supply-base for the legions marching along them.

The necessity of getting units of the Roman army rapidly
from point A to point B had been one of the primary reasons
for the making of roads as long ago as the seventh century
B.C. in the days of the early Roman kings. Later they were

necessary, in any Roman province, for administrative purposes as well. A governor, or the procurator, the Finance Officer at the Treasury, must be able to keep in touch with all districts under his jurisdiction, and though the top speed of even official communications in Roman times was only that of the fastest horse, yet smooth roads free from mud and potholes in winter as well as summer made the best use possible of that equine speed which was never surpassed till the coming of the railways in the third decade of the nineteenth century.

But though Roman roads were made primarily for military and official use anyone could journey on them, civilian travellers and traders as well as soldiers, imperial messengers and government officials—provided, of course, that these non-official persons did not get in the way of more important individuals. Moreover, as legionary auxiliaries patrolled the highways, travel on them was safer during the Roman occupation of Britain than it was to be again until the nineteenth century—unless we accept that somewhat hypothetical interval in the reign of the seventh-century Saxon king, Edwin of Northumbria, when, as Bede tells us, 'which way soever King Edwin's dominions lay a weak woman might have walked with her newborn babe over all the island even from sea to sea without any damage or danger.'

The greatest of the Roman roads in Britain still exist, though their original features have long since been obliterated. Though they were allowed to fall into disrepair and decay in the twilight of civilization when the Saxons came they never entirely disappeared, and were used throughout the so-called 'Dark' and Middle Ages, miry and rutted though they had become. Nowadays, of course, the Roman foundations lie far down beneath modern levels and macadamizing. Sometimes, however, when modern roads have deserted the ancient routes, the original Roman road may still be seen, even if only patchily. So we may stand upon a stretch of actual Roman road—Stane Street—running over the chalk Downs of Sussex above Bignor; it went from Noviomagus Regnensum (Chichester) and made straight through Hardham and Ewell (in modern terms) to Londinium. Or we may see, at Blackpool Bridge in the

Forest of Dean, the broken paving of the original Roman
road, tufted now with grass in nooks and crannies as it runs
among the trees. Or in a more uninhabited and desolate
area we may get a deeper impression of the past as we stand
on the shattered surface of the former Roman military road,
now forsaken and indeed impassable except by pedestrians,
over Wheeldale Moor above Goathland in Yorkshire.

But most of the Roman highways are now motor-roads.
Their names—Watling Street, Ermine Street, Stane Street,
Akeman Street—were given to them in Saxon times. What
the Romans called them, if anything, we do not know; but
as the highways of ancient Italy all had Roman names—
the Appian Way, the Flaminian Way, the Aemilian Way—it
is reasonable to suppose that our British highways had
Roman names too. But if so it is one of those things that
lie buried under the ruins of the collapse of Roman Britain
in the fifth century. The Saxon word 'straet' is, of course,
the invaders' version of the Roman *via strata*, which means a
levelled, 'laid down' or surfaced way. Perhaps the Saxons
learnt the term from the Latin-speaking Britons whom they
subjugated, as they learnt the word *castra*, a (Roman) camp,
which became chester or cester in the Saxon tongue. More
than that we cannot with certainty say.

Watling Street—for convenience we call these roads by
their mediaeval names—ran from Rutupiae, the port of
entry into Britain on the Isle of Thanet, through Duro-
vernum (Canterbury) north-westerly to the Medway valley
at Durobrivae (Rochester) to Londinium, thence north-
westerly still to Deva (Chester) touching Viroconium
(Wroxeter) on the way; the Kentish part of it being, we note,
the route taken by Aulus Plautius on his march in A.D. 43.
This road (much modernized, needless to say) is still in use
along almost its whole length from London to Wroxeter,
showing how well the Romans sited their roads. Ermine
Street went north by an easterly route to Castor on the
Nene, skirting the Fens to Lindum Colonia (the original,
though not the final, legionary fortress of the Ninth).
Westerly from Londinium ran the Akeman Way; it joined
Calleva (Silchester, now only a village) Corinium (Ciren-
cester) and Glevum (Gloucester) and went onwards as the

c

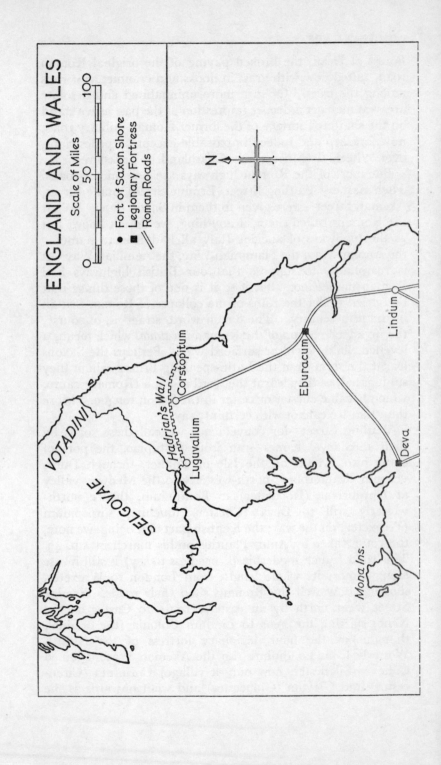

ENGLAND AND WALES

Scale of Miles

0   50   100

● Fort of Saxon Shore
■ Legionary Fortress
// Roman Roads

N

VOTADINI

SELGOVAE

Hadrian's Wall

Luguvalium

Corstopitum

Eburacum

Deva

Lindum

Mona Ins.

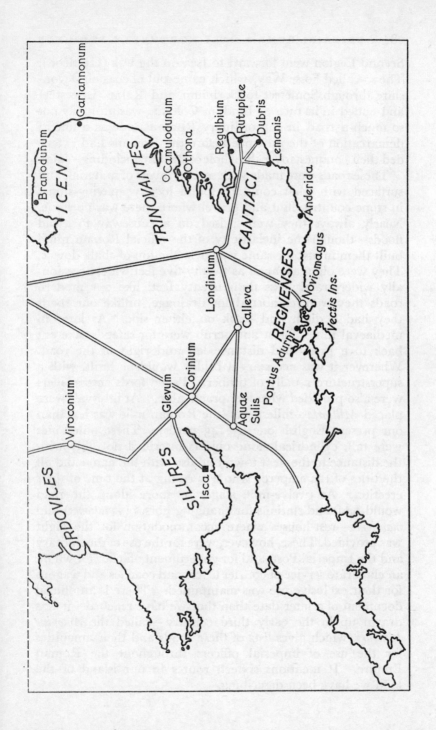

Second Legion went forward to Isca on the Usk (Caerleon). The so-called Fosse Way, which came out of coastal Devonshire through Somerset to Corinium and Ratae (Leicester) and ended in its turn at Lindum Colonia, was probably not so much a road in the ordinary Roman sense as a line of demarcation of the province before the Romans had extended their conquests over the whole of Britain, including Wales.

These roads were made with several layers of material, and surfaced with what could be found locally—paving-stones in stone country, flint and gravel where there was no stone. Nearly always they were raised on a causeway to avoid floods—though the inelasticity of the official Roman mind built them in just the same way over the top of chalk downs. They were often as much as twenty-five feet wide, occasionally wider, rarely less than twenty feet; like our modern roads they were cambered for drainage, unlike our roads they had a ditch and bank on either side. As later in mediaeval times, forest and scrub were for safety's sake cut back to a prescribed distance left and right of the road. Wherever it was necessary a bridge would be built, with a superstructure usually of timber. Paved fords across rivers were also provided wherever practicable. At intervals were placed *Milliaria*—milestones (the Roman mile was less than our present English one by 143 yards). These milestones were tall, cylindrical stone objects inscribed not only with the distance to the next town but also with the name and all the titles of the emperor who was ruling at the time of their erection. At twelve-mile stages or more along the road would be found stations for changing horses (*mutationes*) and *mansiones*—rest-houses where accommodation for the night was provided. These, however, were for the use of the military and the Imperial Post, and for government officials for whom an elaborate service of courier litters and coaches and wagons for their exclusive use was maintained. There is an official document of a later date than that we have reached—it was drawn up in the early third century—called the *Antonine Itinerary*, which gives lists of these roads and their amenities for the use of imperial officers throughout the Roman Empire. It mentions sixteen routes in our island of the kind we have been describing.

There are in Britain about 5,000 miles of Roman roads
known to us today. They appear on maps of Roman Britain
spreading out like a net on all sides from London, and if we
study that net closely we see that the Romans deliberately
designed their road system to connect the *coloniae*, the
legionary fortresses and the tribal capitals (of which more
later). There were trunk roads necessary for provincial
communication and strategy, and there were also secondary
roads (B roads, as we might say now, good, but not quite so
good) which opened up the territory of the canton and linked
its minor administrative centres. Thus the Roman government had the means of speedy access— since Roman
surveyors always sought the shortest, that is, the straightest,
way between two points for their roads—to all centres, civil
and military. No part of the land, once the roads had been
driven across it, would be out of government reach.

Who paid for the making and upkeep of these arteries of
communication? Such main roads as were laid out by the
central government were built by labour gangs provided by
the natives of the tribal cantons through which they were to
pass; these worked under the supervision of Roman military
engineers. The upkeep of the secondary or cantonal roads
fell upon the tribal communities of the neighbourhood. And
if you ask who paid for the upkeep of the Imperial Post, and
the changing stations and rest-houses, and the fuel to keep
the rest-houses warm in winter and to cook the food in all
seasons, the answer is still, the communities where the service
operated. Unlike our modern Post, which we do indeed pay
for, but which operates for the public benefit, the Roman
Imperial Post operated at the public expense for the use of
the government only. If you were a private individual and
wanted to get a message from, say, Noviomagus to Calleva
you had to make your own arrangements. Still more
awkward was it for you if you wished to deal in private
traffic with small places a few miles off which the lordly *viae
stratae*, driving directly across country, had left unnoticed at
a distance on either side.

No doubt then you would fall back upon the ancient
Celtic trackways, which remained in use throughout the
Roman period. Most famous of these, trodden out perhaps

four thousand years earlier, was the Icknield Way (still visible in parts and traceable along most of its course). This ran over Salisbury Plain not far to the east of Stonehenge, entered Berkshire above Ashbury, forded the Thames at Wallingford, then, following the ridge of the Chilterns, eventually entered Cambridgeshire; it then passed north-easterly through Newmarket and across the Breckland— significantly near the prehistoric flint mines of Grimes Graves—forded the little Ouse at Thetford and finally, passing Swaffham on the west (where it is now a rural grassy track known as the Peddars Way) crossed the Nar and made for the coast near Hunstanton. Another equally famous track, a 'green road' today, is the Berkshire Ridgeway. This is really an alternative route of the Icknield Way over the heights of the Berkshire Downs; it runs above Wantage and Uffington and the Vale of the White Horse, passing on its way the pre-Roman horse cut in the chalk of the hillside (perhaps the badge of a British tribe of those days), the neolithic ruins of the tomb of sarsen stones called long ago Wayland Smith's cave, and the Iron Age forts of Uffington and Letcome Castles. It has been suggested with some plausibility that the Berkshire Ridgeway along the drier hill-top was for winter use, and the lower Icknield Way for summer journeys. A third famous pre-Roman trackway ran from Salisbury Plain over the Hampshire Downs north of Andover. It passed through Farnham in Surrey, along the elevated ridge of the Hog's Back just west of Guildford, along the top of the North Downs above Dorking and Reigate, then along the southern slopes of those Downs across Kent to reach the east Kent coast. Part of this track was extensively used as late as the Middle Ages by pilgrims journeying from Winchester to Canterbury. In Surrey and in Kent this section is still called 'The Pilgrims' Way'. An aura of antiquity hangs to this day over the lonelier stretches of all these ancient trackways, especially in those parts where they go as prehistoric man chose to go whenever possible: along the tops of the hills, where it was drier underfoot and he could see afar if danger threatened.

In faraway, sparsely inhabited places—or places which were sparsely inhabited then—the Romans did not bother to get all their apparatus of survey and mensuration into operation at all. They themselves also 'made do' with the existing tracks, perhaps setting up a milestone here and there but doing no more. These would naturally be tracks that led to nothing that was important in Roman eyes. We find that this happened seemingly in the far-western lands of the Dumnonii in Devon and Cornwall. This does not surprise us; it is not so very long ago that the farther parts of Cornwall were still considered remote. But we are surprised to find that the middle valleys of the Thames and Severn and certain Midland areas were similarly roadless. For an explanation we have to remember that these areas were in Roman days swampy marshes or dank woodland, where only a thin population of hunters and fishers eked out an existence untouched, or nearly so, by Roman civilization. In dealing with the history of Roman Britain we must never forget that many parts of the land presented an entirely different aspect then from that which they do now.

In dealing thus comprehensively with the Roman roads of Britain we have of necessity covered a stretch of time extending over the whole period of the Occupation. We must now return to the year A.D. 69, known in Roman history as 'the year of the four emperors'. The confusion and strife which followed the death of Nero did not affect anyone in Britain except, for a while, certain of the legionaries; so we may pass over the troubles stirring elsewhere, which ended when Vespasian, whom we met in 43 commanding the Second Legion at Maiden Castle, became emperor, and a new era in the conquest and expansion of Britain began.

V · THE ACTIVITIES OF AGRICOLA

Suetonius had been checked in his advance against the Welsh tribes by the near-disaster of Boudicca's revolt and his subsequent recall to Rome, and nothing more was done to extend the province or subdue the foes on its borders for a decade. The Fourteenth Legion had been recalled by Nero, who had business for it elsewhere; and though it was returned to Britain in 69 and perhaps stationed with the Ninth at Lindum, it was soon withdrawn once more to the Continent, and we never hear of it in Britain again. To take its place another Second Legion was sent over. This was the Second Adjutrix—to be distinguished from the Second which had played its part in the early advance under Vespasian in the days of Aulus Plautius, which was the Second Augusta. Actually the Second Adjutrix was in its turn withdrawn in the time of Domitian, at the end of this first century A.D., and after that Britain was garrisoned at first by three, then at the end by only two legions until the Roman army melted away from the land altogether.

The energetic governor who set things moving again after they had stagnated, more or less, for ten years was Petillius Cerealis, he who had led the Ninth Legion from Lindum to confront Boudicca and her fiery hordes, and who had been disastrously defeated by her. He had, however, lived down this humiliation and won honours in a war against German rebels on the Rhine, so that his appointment in 71 as governor of Britain need cause no surprise, especially as he was a dashing and capable leader, well qualified to carry out a policy of aggrandisement which may have been his own idea, but was more likely to have been that of his master, the Emperor Vespasian. This policy was to extend the boundaries of the province beyond their present precarious line. The existence of the independent Silures and Ordovices along almost the whole western flank of Britain was too dangerous to be allowed to continue; and did not the restless and warlike Brigantes on the northern frontier constitute a perpetual menace to the new province? Both these potential enemies, therefore, must be rendered impotent, otherwise a stable peace would never be secured.

As it happened, Cerealis became embroiled in Brigantian affairs involuntarily. The Brigantian queen, Cartimandua, the same who had surrendered the refugee Caratacus to Ostorius Scapula, the Roman governor, twenty years before, was still quarrelling in 71 as she had been then with her husband Venutius, and only ceased from quarrelling when she abandoned him and married his armour-bearer. At this insult the enraged chieftain immediately called all his Brigantian warriors together to expel his queen and her lover from Brigantian territory. Cartimandua's answer to this move was to ask the Roman governor—she was still pro-Roman—for help. A few Roman cohorts were sent to her aid, but they were nothing to the forces which Venutius had behind him, and all the Romans could do was to bring the queen to a place of safety away from her outraged countrymen. Venutius, unlike his consort, had never been pro-Roman. He was, in fact, the centre of anti-Roman sentiment and resistance to Rome. He had no desire to rob the enemy of his unfaithful queen nor, probably, any interest in what became of her; but she had provided him with as good an excuse as any for open hostility, and he now declared war upon the Romans.

This war was to last, on and off, for fourteen years, and even at the end of that time the Brigantes were not properly subdued till many decades later. No Roman writer gives us precise details of what occurred, but it is clear that the resistance of these wild, embattled tribes of what was to be called in Saxon times Northumbria was stubborn, that though they were often subdued they revolted again at the slightest provocation, and that there were 'many battles and much blood shed before the greater part of the Brigantian territory was either annexed or devastated'. But this is being too sweeping. Certainly at this period all the lands of the Brigantes—that is, the whole area from the Humber to the Tyne–Solway line, were not annexed, though they may have been devastated. The plain of York and parts of

Lancashire were probably meant by 'the greater part of Brigantian territory', while in the wild valleys of that Pennine Range which runs centrally through Brigantia the hard core of resistance was untouched, and the mountains were a stronghold of fierce Brigantian chieftains and their unsubdued, redoubtable warrior-bands.

In short, it seems that Cerealis, for all his dash and energy, was never able during his governorship to force his way right through the territory of the Brigantes to its northern boundary, the Tyne–Solway line—a line we shall hear more of presently. But he did found a northern capital in that territory, on the site of a former Brigantian village, and built a legionary fortress there, to which he moved forward the Ninth Legion from Lindum. This was Eboracum, a name abbreviated in the Middle Ages to York. Lindum, left behind to the southward, now became a *colonia*, and in course of time spread down from its hill to the banks of the river below. Evacuated by the legionaries, it became a place of retirement for the *veterani*. From now on Eboracum, Deva and Isca remained the three great legionary fortresses until the years of declining Roman power in Britain.

Cerealis was not allowed to complete the subjugation of the Brigantes. In 74 he was recalled, his place being taken by Sextus Julius Frontinus.

Frontinus seems to have been about to attempt to complete Cerealis's work amongst the Brigantes. But while his back was turned and he was, they hoped, too busy elsewhere to take much notice of them, the Silures of South Wales appear to have made an incursion into Roman territory. Frontinus immediately turned upon them, leaving the war in the north unfinished, and set about the conquest of the Silures. What Ostorius Scapula had been unable to do Frontinus achieved. The Silures at last submitted. Frontinus planted forts manned by auxiliaries in the heart of Silurian territory, of which traces still remain in the south Welsh hills, but he did not emulate Cerealis in moving a legion forward into the land of the foe. The Second Legion remained on the borders of it, at Isca. A military road (of course) was built from Isca along the south Welsh coast to Nidum (Neath) and Maridunum (Carmarthen), but we cannot be sure whether it was

Frontinus or some later governor who was responsible for its building.

Cerealis and Frontinus each held office as governor of Britain for four years, which was about the normal length of a provincial governor's tenure of office. But the next governor, one of the greatest, or at least the best known to us, Cnaeus Julius Agricola, governed Britain for seven years. We know a good deal about Agricola, the citizen of Forum Julii (Fréjus) in Provence, because he was the father-in-law of the Roman historian Tacitus, who wrote a biography, or rather a panegyric, of his father-in-law, whose undoubted virtues he vigorously emphasized, and whose exploits he unreservedly lauded. In this biography Tacitus does not tell us all we should like to know about the land of Britain. He was not interested in our country, 'where the climate,' he understandably remarks, 'is objectionable, with frequent mists and rains'—though he relents sufficiently to grant that 'there is no extreme cold'. He is interested only in Agricola, and all he says about Britain is merely a background—and one without place-names or topographical details at that—to the exploits of his hero.

Yet he does not give us the intimate, personal details about Agricola to which modern biographies of great men have accustomed us, and which we should much like to have. Even when he says, 'If posterity would like to know what his physical appearance was', all he tells us is that 'he was attractive rather than impressive. His expression was full of charm, but his features lacked forcefulness. You could see immediately that he was a good man, and you were tempted to believe him a great one,' which statements do not help us very much in visualizing him. Tacitus is rather better in dealing with his character. He says that through living his early years and going to school in Massilia (Marseilles) where Greek refinement and the honest simplicity typical of the provinces 'met in a happy blend', he would have been protected from the malign influence of evil companions even if his own honourable instincts had not been as a shield to him. He never boasted of his achievements, and when he was only a subordinate he always gave the credit of any successful action to his leader, as the source of his inspiration.   He was modest in his dress, an affable companion, and had no taste for vast wealth—this last a rare trait in Rome in the days of the emperors.

It was the gruff peasant-emperor Vespasian, bull-necked, rough-mannered and forthright, who had once been dismissed from court because he went to sleep while Nero was singing, but whose reign opened one of the most peaceful and constructive eras of the Roman Empire, who chose Agricola to be governor of Britain after Frontinus.   He chose him for the soundest of reasons: Agricola *knew* Britain— better, probably, than any other Roman then living.   As quite a young man he had served on the staff of Suetonius Paulinus, and must have watched the charge of the legionaries as they drove back the Druids upon their sacrificial fires; he must have been there when the reports were brought in of the firing of Camulodunum and Verulamium by Boudicca, and have been at his side when Paulinus faced the British queen and her tribal hordes and defeated them— grim warfare enough, which, says Tacitus, 'caused his spirit to be invaded by a passion for military glory'.   Then, after an absence of some years, he returned to Britain as legate of the restive, almost mutinous and certainly out-of-hand Twentieth Legion at Deva.   We should like to know exactly how—by what qualities of forbearance or clemency or whatever it was—he eventually gained the legion's obedience, respect and even affection; but once again Tacitus fails us. All he says on the subject is, 'he let it appear that he found in the legion the loyalty he created'—we have to imagine the rest.   Anyhow, he led the Twentieth to play its part successfully with the Ninth when the governor Cerealis advanced against the Brigantians: 'it was hard work and danger that Cerealis shared with Agricola', Tacitus says.

Agricola knew all about Britain's objectionable climate (it was no doubt from him that Tacitus got his information); its grey skies and cold mists and winter frosts and snows; the bleak hills of the north, and the 'northern shores beaten by a wild and open sea', the craggy mountains and waterfalls tumbling from a height in Wales, the desolate Yorkshire moors, windswept and rainbeaten; he also knew the difference there was between the gentle, peaceful south and the warlike, forbidding north; and in his seven years in Britain he achieved much, both in the arts of war and those of peace —the latter more permanent than many of the former.

On arriving in Britain as governor, probably just after midsummer in the year 78, Agricola first of all turned his attention to the Ordovices, the still unsubdued inhabitants of North Wales, who had recently wiped out a squadron of Roman cavalry stationed in their land. Agricola led his troops into the heart of the mountains—a fearful risk— inspiring with courage those he commanded by proving his own as he went forward in the van. As a result of this bold move he disastrously defeated the enemy in their own territory. But far from resting on his laurels he decided, although the campaigning season was drawing to a close, to reduce Anglesey—it will be remembered that Boudicca's revolt had prevented Paulinus from completing the occupation of that island. As, owing to the lateness of the season, he had decided on swift action Agricola, unlike Paulinus, had no ships at hand, so he ordered specially chosen auxiliaries, trained in what we should now call commando work, to swim under arms and with their horses under control swimming beside them, across the Menai Strait at low tide and attack the tribesmen, assembled once again as they had been seventeen years before, in their sacred island. At this the Ordovices, taken completely by surprise, for they had expected ships and a naval engagement, lost their heads. 'What could embarrass or defeat a foe who attacked like that?' Tacitus imagines them asking each other. So they sued for peace, and surrendered their holy Mona; and this was the end of trouble from the Welsh tribes. However, Agricola seems not to have trusted the Welsh entirely, for the Twentieth Legion remained at Deva to keep an eye on the Ordovices in the north, and the Second remained watching the Silures in the south.

For two years after this Agricola, in a pause before the great operation of his term of office in Britain, devoted his energies to the reorganization of the administration of the province. Further, he was bent on persuading the Britons, or at any rate the Britons of the more peaceful and amenable south, to adopt the amenities of Roman civilization; to 'romanize' them as the Gauls and Spaniards had been romanized, or as Tacitus, not without cynicism, puts it, 'to persuade a people scattered and uncivilized before, and on that account pugnacious, to grow pleasurably inured to peace and ease'. Neither Greeks nor Romans could understand civilization divorced from town-life. Their civilization was an urban one. On the other hand the Britons, like the Saxons who were to come after them, preferred a rural existence. Agricola's policy was to wean them from their old rustic tribal life, and the jealousies and inter-tribal strife to which it led, and to settle them in towns. He directed his military engineers to design such towns for the natives, taking care to site them in localities that had hitherto been centres of tribal influence—the place where a British chieftain had had his stronghold, if possible, a former rallying point of the tribe which would hold strong associations and traditions for them. Then they were to teach the natives how to build in brick and stone along an alignment of streets on a grid-pattern, similar in lay-out to the streets of a military camp. Thus, although such Britons as herdsmen and shepherds and peasants generally were for the most part untouched by this stream of romanization, a new kind of life began for a great part of the people.

Tacitus's opinion was that the Britons submitted to the levy, the tribute and the other charges of Empire with cheerful readiness, so long as they were not made the victims of abuse; 'they were broken in to obedience, but not to slavery'. Indeed, they seem to have thought that the burden of taxation which was the price of the benefits of the Roman occupation was preferable to the only alternative—inter-tribal anarchy, which had hitherto prevented them from co-operating and so had made them an easy prey to a disciplined invader. Realizing that conquest followed by oppressive administration could only lead, as in Boudicca's case, to dangerous revolt, Agricola took great care to end any abuses that might cause resentment leading inevitably to rebellion among such provincials as these. One of the greatest benefits he bestowed upon the Britons was the purification during his term of office of the civil service. We have seen what damage the petty officials of the Treasury and of the governor's staff did amongst the Iceni in 60 and 61. Agricola sharpened his sword against such offenders, and by dealing with them as they deserved banished the greater grievances that had afflicted the people. Tacitus tells us that he made no use of freedmen or slaves for official business. He preferred to appoint to official positions and duties men whom he could trust not to transgress, rather than to punish transgressors. And beginning with himself and his staff, he enforced discipline in his own household first.

He then persuaded the British chieftains to allow their sons to be 'trained in the liberal arts'—that is, to be educated in Roman and Greek literature, philosophy and rhetoric —and discovered that the Britons, formerly considered barbarians, showed 'great natural ability'. The consequence of all this was, eventually, that instead of showing resentment at the presence of the conquerors, the Britons, while still keeping their old Celtic tongue, began to speak and write Latin as well. In fact, the ability to speak Latin, and the wearing of the toga, the Roman national dress, became among the Britons (always excluding the peasants) what we should call nowadays a 'status symbol'. It seems, too, that it was during the governorship of Agricola that intermarriage of Britons and Romans began.

We have noted how Tacitus affirms that after serving in his youth on Paulinus's staff 'Agricola's spirit was invaded by a passion for military glory'; and the great achievement he set himself during the years he was governor of Britain was nothing less than the conquest of the far north—Scotland, the land of Caledonia. But before he could set his hand to this formidable task, considering the nature of the country he proposed invading, he had to complete the conquest of the territory of the Brigantes, the unpeaceful and far from amenable north, left unfinished by Cerealis and Frontinus. Tacitus is so vague in his account of Agricola's doings in the north, up to the Tyne–Solway line, telling us only, without mentioning any names, that 'he left no part of hostile territory undisturbed, but ravaged it by sudden incursions, and by encompassing the Brigantes with garrisons and forts', that we are unable to form a detailed picture of what Agricola

really did do. We are, however, given to understand that
'when he had struck sufficient terror into the souls of the
enemy he wooed them to submission by his clemency, and
many states which had till then maintained their independence abandoned their resentful mood and accepted the
curb of garrisons and forts'.

Agricola then seems to have established a line of forts
between the Solway and the Tyne—where the great Wall of
Hadrian was to be built just over forty years later; and this
fortified line certainly 'encompassed' the Brigantes and might
have been considered (as Hadrian afterwards considered it)
a good final boundary for the province. But Agricola had
other ideas. Greatly daring, considering that the Brigantes
had only just been subdued and might at a moment's notice
or no notice at all revolt, and that his base at Eboracum
already lay eighty miles to the south, he pushed on into the
Lowlands, and reached the narrow neck of land between the
Clyde and the Forth.

It was fortunate for Agricola that the Brigantes he had
left in his rear were either cowed or exhausted or possibly
both by his campaigns against them, for if they had chosen
to rise behind him while he was leading the bulk of his
troops into the wilds of Caledonia in the years 80 to 84
disaster must have overtaken him. Even as it was Agricola
had overambitiously undertaken a project for which he had
not sufficient forces. On his advance into Galloway, he
even looked acquisitively across the sea in the direction of
Ireland, and even considered (says Tacitus) that that island
'could be reduced and held by a single legion and a few
auxiliaries'! However, mercifully for his reputation, he
thought better of it and left Ireland alone. Eire was
destined to be immune from invasion until the days of the
Vikings and the Norman kings of England. In fact, as the
decades slipped by it was the Irish (called in those days
Scotti) who invaded Roman Britain, not the Romans who
invaded Ireland.

In 83 began Agricola's great offensive against Scotland.
His strategy was to advance by the eastern route over the
Lothian Plain while his fleet sailed approximately parallel
to the marching column, raiding and threatening potential

trouble-spots on the coast; to block with a fort every valley-entrance into the Highlands on his left down which the enemy might advance to attack his lines of communication, and so to reach Aberdeenshire; and as an attack upon the formidable Highlands was too perilous an undertaking his idea was to blockade this mountainous massif.

His route may be followed by means of the forts which have been excavated and dated by archaeologists on the western side of the Lothian Plain from the Firth of Forth to the crossing of the river below Stirling, then westwards of the Ochil Hills to Ardoch. From there he headed north-east and planted forts at Strageath and Gask; he had planted them also in the valley entrances at Bochastle, Dalginross and Fendoch. Here that part of his army which was composed of the Ninth Legion—a weak spot, because that legion's ranks had been depleted to furnish vexillations for Domitian's German War—was attacked by night by Caledonian tribesmen and might have been disastrously overwhelmed if Agricola had not come to its aid in time and decisively defeated the foe. Then advancing up Strathmore he planted on the Tay, at the spot where it leaves the Highlands, the great fortress of Inchtuthill—well excavated in 1952 by Professor Richmond. This is the most northerly permanent Roman station (as distinct from temporary marching camps), of the period. The camps continue at approximately twelve-mile intervals almost to the Moray Firth, and end at Fochabers by Elgin.

In the following summer came the last of Agricola's great offensive campaigns. 'All the tribes that inhabit Caledonia' —the warriors 'with reddish hair and large limbs'—had now united in one great host to confront Agricola's forces: foot-soldiers, charioteers and horsemen, who, having sent non-combatants with their cattle up into the more remote valleys had bound themselves by oaths and sacrifices to their gods to stand together and drive out the invader. There are said—almost certainly with exaggeration—to have been 30,000 of them. The battle was fought where the foothills of a range of high mountains come down to the plain. Tacitus calls the spot 'Mons Graupius', but gives us no topographical details to enable us to determine exactly

D

SCOTLAND

Scale of miles

0   50   100

Agricola's possible invasion route ·—··—·
and the line of the Antonine Wall

ORKNEY

Moray Firth

Elgin

Strath Spey

CALEDONES

GRAMPIANS

ABERDEENSHIRE

SKYE

Inchtuthill

R. Tay

Strathmore

Fendoch

Strageath

Dalginross

Ardoch

Gask

Ochil Hills

Firth of Tay

Firth of Forth

MULL

Stirling

Antonine Wall

LOTHIANS

Berwick

R. Tweed

Trimontium

KINTYRE

ARRAN

N

CHEVIOTS

Bremenium

To Hadrian's Wall

where 'Mons Graupius' was. Unfortunately, therefore, the spot where Agricola inflicted a major defeat on the Caledonians cannot be identified.

It proved an indecisive defeat, however. The Caledonians withdrew into the high mountains, obviously determined on continuing the war. The onset of the northern winter prevented Agricola from following them. He merely directed his fleet—Agricola was the first to form a fleet for Britain; we shall hear more of this *Classis Britannica* later—to sail round the northern end of Britain and return by the Irish Sea and the Channel, and himself withdrew to winter quarters. Undoubtedly he had intended renewing the war when the campaigning season of 85 opened, but before that time came he was recalled to Rome by the emperor Domitian, the younger son of Vespasian. Vespasian himself, and Titus, his elder son only for a brief time emperor, were both now dead.

Tacitus gives the reason for Agricola's recall as Domitian's jealousy of the triumphant general; but though the unattractive tyrant Domitian very likely was jealous, his real reason for the recall was probably first, that Agricola's campaigns were becoming too grandiose and expensive in men and money for what they achieved—after four years the war against the Caledonians was still not finally won—and second, that Domitian had wars on hand on the Continent which needed troops that in his opinion could be better employed than fighting in the unimportant territory of northern Britain.

Agricola ended his days in retirement in Rome—he never saw Britain again, and died in A.D. 93. His son-in-law concludes his biography with words worth quoting:

> If there is any abiding-place for the spirits of the just, if, as philosophers affirm, noble souls do not die with the mortal body, quiet, O Father, may you rest! . . . Everything that won our admiring love in Agricola lives on, and shall live on in men's hearts through endless ages, in the chronicles of fame. Agricola's story has been told to those who shall come hereafter, and by that he will live forever.

Agricola was not an exceptional man—no Alexander, or Caesar, or Napoleon; but he was typical of the better sort of official who came to the fore in the best period of the Roman Empire. He was one of many who helped to build the peaceful, civilized and cultivated South Britain of the century which came after he laid down his office and departed. Romanization of Britain had of course begun before the days of Agricola; but he hastened its progress by his personal encouragement and help, and when all is said that side of his labours for the province that he governed so well for seven years left a more abiding legacy than the impermanent military glory for which he strove in remote Caledonia.

VI · HADRIAN'S WALL

With Agricola's recall the Roman advance into Scotland stopped dead. His victory at Mons Graupius, wherever in the Highlands that may have been, was never followed up, and the Romans never with aggressive designs penetrated into the heart of Caledonia again. As far as the remote north was concerned, as matters afterwards turned out, Agricola would seem during his term of office to have wasted his energies and his time.

No Roman historian chronicled the wars that took place in the more northerly parts of Britain during the later years of Domitian's reign, or those of the successor to Nerva, the Spaniard Trajan. Our knowledge of what happened in these years has to be based mostly on the labours of archaeologists, who work out from the excavation of Roman forts in these parts whether they were destroyed at this period or not, whether they show evidence of having been rebuilt after destruction and reoccupied before being destroyed again; whether there are any inscriptions on them which furnish the names of their builders, or the forces which garrisoned them, and when. They also discover and read the language of the coins which the Romans seem to have dropped prodigally about them; these reveal how long, approximately, such and such a place was occupied by them, for when coins cease, we may be very sure no Roman was any longer about to lose them. Knowledge gained by such means is not, of course, as clear-cut and incontrovertible as that gained from contemporary written records. It cannot be so sharply in focus. It is like a landscape seen behind a mist, shapes glimpsed only in dim outline, no details being visible. Nevertheless, though archaeology sometimes raises more problems and questions than it settles, it furnishes clues to sharp-eyed, trained detectives which often enable them to track down the truth.

So by these means, and these only, we know that the

Romans kept a hold upon the Lowlands, at that time all the land between the Solway–Tyne and the Clyde–Forth, for about thirty years after Agricola had gone, for some of the military stations he established show evidence of having been destroyed but then rebuilt and reoccupied before they were a second time overrun. It appears that the Roman grip upon the Lowlands tightened or relaxed according to whether the untamed and still resentful Brigantes were in revolt or not. Whenever the Caledonians beyond the Forth–Clyde line attacked Agricola's garrisons in the Lowlands and the Romans were dealing with the situation, the Brigantes seem to have seized the opportunity to revolt for which they were always on the lookout, and forced the Romans to turn back from the one troubled situation to confront another, equally dangerous. This, however, is supposition. What is certain is that there was unrest and disturbance throughout the reigns of Domitian and Trajan in all those lands, including Brigantia, which Agricola had recently so laboriously conquered—except, curiously enough, Wales. The fact that detachments were then and afterwards drawn from the Second Legion at Isca to help in the fighting in Brigantia is proof that there could not have been trouble in the lands of the Silures, or soldiers on guard at Isca could not have been spared from their posts. Nor is there any evidence at this time of any risings among the Ordovices. And in the south of Britain the peace that had been established after Boudicca's revolt remained serenely unbroken.

But any Roman official sent as governor to Britain during the years 85 to 120 could hardly have thought himself in luck. He must have been wearily and more often than not unsuccessfully fighting against the Brigantes between the Ouse and the Mersey, and among the thickly strewn forts that Agricola had planted in the Pennine valleys and those he had built between Tyne and Solway, or engaging with the tribes who inhabited the regions north of the Tyne—the Votadini, Selgovae and Novantae—without intermission.

By the year 120 it seems that these last territories—all the lands between the Tyne and the Forth—had been lost by the Romans. Moreover—though we grope among shadows

here—some great catastrophe had apparently overtaken the
Ninth Legion, advancing, in the year 119 or 120, one
supposes, from the legionary fortress at Eboracum to quell a
more than usually virulent uprising of the surrounding
Brigantes. This presumed uprising and the likewise presumed and certainly unrecorded battle to which it led engulfs
the Ninth Legion, and in the profound darkness it completely
disappears. It seems strange that a disaster of such magnitude should have escaped the notice of all Roman historians
except for a passing reference in Fronto's *de bello Parthico* (why
in a work dealing with a war in Parthia, we wonder?) which
states that 'a great number of soldiers were killed by the
Britons in the reign of Hadrian'; but such is the fact. The
end of the Ninth Legion is still, to us, a mystery. A report
of what happened, though, was evidently sent to Rome, and
the situation appeared serious enough to bring over the
emperor himself, in person, to assess the damage and see
what could be done to remedy it. Trajan was now dead,
and the emperor in A.D. 120 was Hadrian.

Unlike Trajan, who was first and foremost a soldier, with
no taste for literature or the arts, Hadrian was by tempera-
ment and inclination a poet and artist. He actually wrote
some poetry, and is said to have attempted painting. He
was so interested in all things Greek—literature, sculpture,
architecture and above all philosophy—that he was nick-
named 'the Greekling'. His restless curiosity urged him on
to cover wide fields, ranging from the oriental mystery
religions to antiquities—had he lived today he would have
been an archaeologist. It spurred him on to see everything
there was to see, and as far as possible to do all there was to
be done. But though his tastes were not primarily political
and certainly not military, nor would he have chosen to be
the administrator of the greatest empire the world had ever
known, when destiny summoned him to be emperor his
sense of duty bade him leave the real passions of his spirit to
such leisure hours as his great office vouchsafed him, and
devote himself to the hard work and thankless task of
government. He had not Trajan's urge for annexation of
such lands as could be conquered by military might; but he
was intensely interested in the already existing provinces of

the Roman Empire, interested in them and deeply sympa-
thetic towards them.   When he became emperor he took the
trouble to see them for himself.   He visited them all in
person, travelling about in them to such an extent that he
was hardly ever in Rome; less than a third part of his reign
of twenty-one years was spent anywhere on Italian soil.   He
had the welfare of the provinces very much at heart; he was
perhaps the first Roman emperor to hold the view that the
provinces did not exist merely for the benefit and glory of
Rome, but had a life of their own and needs and privileges
which ought to be acknowledged by Roman officials.   They
must, of course, submit to the maintenance of military forces
in them; but Hadrian held that armies were there, in the
provinces, only to ensure provincial prosperity and the
safety of provincial frontiers.

Hadrian is one of the more admirable of Roman emperors.
It is fitting that it should be he who left behind him in
Britain our noblest remaining monument of Roman dominion in the land; it is fortunate that we possess, dredged up
from the Thames, the bronze head of a vanished colossal
statue of him (now in the British Museum) which gives us an
idea of what he looked like.   And it is typical of the man that
when he received news of the disastrous state of affairs in
northern Britain in the year 120 he should come in person to
deal with the situation, probably bringing with him a new
legion—the Sixth—to fill the place of the vanished Ninth.
The Sixth Legion is recorded as having been transferred from
the Rhine to Britain about this time, so it is certain that if it
did not actually accompany the emperor on his journey it
arrived soon after—and stayed at Eboracum until, three
hundred years later, the Romans finally departed out of the
land.

Unfortunately there is no contemporary account of
Hadrian's doings in Britain, but we can guess how he
occupied his time there by what happened after he had left
the province.   He had, of course, to reorganize the army,
depleted by the loss of the Ninth Legion, he had to see the
Sixth settled in at the legionary fortress of Eboracum; and he
had to take measures for the repression of the Brigantian
revolt and the prevention of such revolts in the future.   How

to deal with these troublesome Brigantes? That was the question. He 'walked about Britain' (as his friend Florus put it) both to see what had been done in the past by Agricola, and what could be done in the future by himself. He evidently surveyed the line of forts which Agricola had built to 'encompass' the Brigantes between the years 80 and 82; these, we remember, were strung out between Tyne and Solway, over a distance of seventy-two miles; whether any of them were still garrisoned or not we have no means of knowing. As usual, a military road had been built by Agricola's engineers joining them (we call it now the Stanegate) to ensure speedy communications, but Hadrian laid his finger at once on the flaw in Agricola's 'encompassing' arrangements, which had made them inadequate to restrain the revolting Brigantes. They were detached forts, around which and between which an enemy could easily pass, and through the gaps between them help could speedily come to any rebels seeking it from the lands farther north.

So to overcome this weakness Hadrian conceived the idea of superseding the detached Agricolan forts by erecting a continuous stone wall furnished with a rampart walk, signalling turrets, and fortlets to accommodate a vigilant patrol continuously watching hostile territory. North of this there was to be a deep ditch, except where the Wall ran along the summit of precipitous escarpments like the Whin Sill, which at Winshields is 1,230 feet above sea-level and the highest point to which the Wall rises; or where, as on its flanks, it faced the sea. A ditch in these cases would of course have been unnecessary. On the Wall itself the fortlets (now called milecastles) were to be placed at each Roman mile (about 1,620 yards) and between each milecastle and the next there were to be two equidistant turrets to house the signallers. A broad, flat-bottomed ditch, rather inaptly called in later times the Vallum (which really means a rampart, not a ditch) ran south of the Wall, and naturally there would be a military road, also on the south, for communications and the transmission of supplies. Opinions differ about the date and the function of the Vallum, some scholars ascribing it to the years before Hadrian's arrival on the scene, others thinking it was made after his time, and its purpose, according to the many current opinions, varies from a sort of customs barrier to a kind of Roman Offa's Dyke, marking the frontier and clearly showing where the Roman province ended and hostile territory began. (The latter suggestion is probably nearer the truth.) In any case, whatever its purpose was, it appears soon to have gone out of use, so let us concentrate our attention upon the actual Wall.

It stretches for 80 Roman, 72 English, miles from Wallsend on Tyne east of Newcastle to Bowness on Solway, west of Carlisle. Early writers from Bede in the eighth century to Camden, the Elizabethan antiquary, in the late sixteenth, thought that while the Vallum was a frontier-work of Hadrian's, the stone Wall was built nearly eighty years later by the emperor Severus; but modern excavation has now confirmed the nineteenth-century view that the Wall was Hadrian's work, though there were several changes of his original plan before it was completed. It was, for instance, originally intended to be ten Roman feet wide, and foundations along practically the whole line were laid down on that assumption; but after only a part of the Wall had been built upon them the width was reduced—probably for economy in labour as well as expense—to eight feet. Accordingly, we now see in several places the wide foundation projecting like a massive ledge at the base of the narrower Wall. Another change of plan involved the western, Cumberland, part of the Wall, which was first made of turf cut and laid like brickwork: not long after its erection in this material the turf was replaced by stone. Even more radical than these details was the fact that during the course of the building the strategy of the Wall appears to have been changed. Hadrian seems to have envisaged the Wall as merely a patrol walk; the fighting, as distinct from the patrolling garrison was not to be *on* the Wall, but close at hand behind it, in forts south of the patrol line. No doubt his idea had been to use Agricola's already existing forts on the Stanegate for its accommodation. For excavation has shown that the large forts now incorporated in the Wall were built after the foundations had been laid, taking no account of them; so soon, however, after the Wall had been begun as to give rise to the

supposition that the change of plan indicated the existence of
fierce and resentful opposition to the new barrier among the
Lowland tribes who saw in it a preposterous curb to their
expeditions into Roman territory. Not only, therefore,
were the forts placed on the Wall itself, but outpost forts
were also built in Lowland areas north of the Wall to give
early warning of attacks that were evidently growing
extremely menacing even while the Wall was in course of
erection.

It must be understood that the Wall now called the
'Roman Wall', or more often 'Hadrian's Wall', was never
meant to be a fighting platform. It was merely, as one
authority has called it,[1] 'an elevated sentry-walk'. The
fighting garrison, when attacks materialized, would emerge
from the north gate of their fort, which opened into enemy
territory, and helped if necessary by the men sallying from
the north gates of the milecastles, would advance into the
open and fight in the manner in which the Roman army was
trained to fight, in formation with spears and swords, in the
field, their aim being to roll up the attackers against the
barrier they were intending to cross. But though it was no
fighting platform, it could be an effective obstacle to raiding
parties because, although determined foes could comparatively easily mount it and cross it, once across they
would find themselves caught, for while it was garrisoned
and patrolled it would have been practically impossible for
them to get themselves and their loot back across it again.

How high, then, was this barrier? Bede, in 731, when far
more of the Wall was still to be seen than is visible today,
says that it was eight feet wide and twelve feet high. But
Bede never travelled outside his own monastery at Jarrow,
on the Tyne opposite Wallsend, so he is obviously talking
about only that part of the Wall which survived in his
own neighbourhood. Sixteenth-century writers, who went
farther afield, described it as being higher—up to fifteen feet
in their time. Nowadays there is only one small piece at
Hare Hill near Banks Turret in Cumberland which reaches
nine feet ten inches; apart from this fragment—and partly a
nineteenth-century restoration at that—in its best preserved

[1] Collingwood.

parts its present height barely averages six feet. Probably originally it was fifteen feet to the rampart walk, and with a six-foot embattled parapet above that it would reach a height of over twenty feet.

It had a core of lime-concrete made with rough stones and mortar and was faced on both sides with ashlar. This, of course, we can still see with our own eyes as we follow its course as it seems to leap across the country, aiming straight at the most commanding heights, changing direction on lofty points, and abandoning a straight for a re-entrant course only where the crags on which it runs are broken by natural gaps which it enfilades in an easier descent. 'Verily,' says Camden, while Elizabeth I was reigning, 'I have seen the tract of it over the high pitches and steep descents of hilles, wonderfully rising and falling.' The most impressive remains today run from Sewingshields Crags, over Winshields where the Wall majestically

> . . . strides from hill to hill
> Along the wave-crest of the Great Whin Sill,

to the Cawfields milecastle, where modern industry's needs have destroyed it in the midst of one of its noblest stretches—for the ruins we see now are by no means continuous. Quarrying has blasted it away in some places; the motor-road from Newcastle to Carlisle runs for nineteen miles at its eastern end over its foundations, completely obliterating them (except for a short span at Haddon-on-the-Wall); for miles in certain areas it has been quite uprooted, in others (as near the Nine Nicks of Thirlwall) only its foundations are visible, resembling the fossilized backbone of some prehistoric reptile snaking its way over the ups and downs of the rough, wild landscape.

Who were the labourers who raised it? The answer to that is unambiguous. It was detachments brought from all the three legions in Britain who raised it, for every legion of the Roman army contained trained masons as well as engineers, carpenters and armourers. They built it while auxiliary troops formed a fighting cover for them as they did so. We know from inscriptions on stones built into the Wall that the work was partitioned out in lengths of between

35 and 40 yards to individual centuries of the legions; after building one short section, the completion of which was marked by a stone, now called a centurial stone, inscribed with the name of the century, that century moved on to another section prescribed for it elsewhere.

A few of the sixteen forts of the Wall have been excavated, and are now presented to us in a bruised and battered condition that demands much imagination if we are to picture them as they were in their prime. The outlines, and in some cases parts of the gateways, of some milecastles also exist; the lower courses of the walls of several turrets remain, and at Banks Turret, far to the west, from which in favourable weather one may see the distant mountains of Lakeland and the Solway beyond them, the walls rise on one side to a considerable height, with the ruins of the turret's superstructure, which fell long ago, embedded in the ground nearby. Signs of the steps which once led up to the wallwalk are also traceable in this turret.

Yet though its ruins are so fragmentary, even now, when its day is done and its labours long past, the Wall is impressive. It is doubly so when we remember the enormous amount of labour that was involved in its erection, some of it in wild and precipitous country. Moreover, there were bridges to be built over the becks and rivers which the Wall encountered on its way; and all this was in the face of the violence of the elements in northern winters and the bitter opposition in every season of the native tribes not passively looking on, we may be sure, as this great barrier grew before their eyes.

Having made clear his wishes and given his commands after surveying the land the Wall was to traverse, Hadrian left Britain in 121. The building of the Wall became the responsibility of the governor, Aulus Plaetorius Nepos, a former companion and close friend of the emperor's. We know from inscriptions that the work was completed round about A.D. 128. When all was finished the legions returned to their bases, and the auxiliaries—troops composed exclusively of provincials from all quarters of the Roman Empire—were left to garrison it, under Roman officers.

VII · THE ANTONINE WALL

At this line where Hadrian had drawn it the frontier of the province stood unmoved till the year 140 or 141. Then, when a certain Lollius Urbicus was governor of Britain—Antoninus Pius being now emperor in Rome—it was suddenly carried forward again. Once more the Lowlands which Agricola had conquered, or thought he had, sixty years before, and from which the Romans had subsequently withdrawn, were marched over by Roman troops.

Why this sudden forward move after the Hadrianic recession? There seems to have been superficial quiet amongst the Brigantes at this time, and lured on by this the Romans may have thought it possible to extend the frontier to what they might consider a more logical boundary line. But it is more likely that the tribes between the Solway–Tyne and Clyde–Forth, the Votadini, Novantae and Selgovae, were troubling the province. They certainly were troubling the Wall, which plainly roused in the tribesmen, shut out by it from their former plunder grounds, the bitterest resentment. It is quite possible that the Romans thought that the only way to end pressure on the Wall was to advance against and subjugate those who were exerting it. And possibly too they may have considered that as they had tamed the Brigantes (as they imagined) by 'encompassing' them with a wall, so they might tame the Lowland tribes with another wall. We cannot say for certain. The only reference we get to happenings in northern Britain in these years is a sentence in Julius Capitolinus's biography of Antoninus Pius which states: 'Through his legate Lollius Urbicus he [Antoninus] conquered the Britons, and after building another wall, of turf, drove off the barbarians.'

This turf wall across the narrow neck of land between the Clyde and the Forth, 'the place where Britain is narrowest from ocean to ocean', is now known as the Antonine Wall, because it was erected in the reign of Antoninus. Its life

was short, as we shall see, its remains are scantier, as we
should expect, than those of Hadrian's Wall.   Lollius took
detachments from all three of the legions in Britain and from
the Wall garrisons, marched across the territory of the Lowland tribes, seized that narrow neck of land, about thirty-
seven miles wide, and built the turf wall, with nineteen forts
(as against sixteen for the seventy-three miles of Hadrian's
Wall) and a very deep ditch, from Carriden on Forth to Old
Kilpatrick on the Clyde.

The Antonine Wall differed in several respects from the
Wall of Hadrian.   It was of turf (in the eastern parts of clay)
not of stone; it had no rearward vallum, no milecastles and
no turrets, and its forts were generally smaller than those on
Hadrian's Wall, and of course closer together, since nineteen
had to be fitted into a length of only thirty-seven miles.
Furthermore it was not protected on its flanks as was the more
southerly wall—perhaps, it has been suggested, because it
was intended to keep the Lowland tribes in rather than
to keep enemies out.   A great military road starting at
Corstopitum (Corbridge on the Tyne, two miles south of
Hadrian's Wall, an armoury and supply depôt for the garrisons on the Wall) and running to Abercorn on Forth joined
the Antonine Wall to its southern bases in Northumberland.
Along this were built large forts at Habitancum (Risingham)
Bremenium (High Rochester) and Trimontium (Newstead);
remains of all these have been excavated.   This was on the
east.   On the west a similar road must have been planned,
but if so it was never completed.

It is not very clear what the status of Hadrian's Wall was
immediately after the erection of the more northerly wall.
It may have ceased at that time to be patrolled; the garrisons
seem to have been withdrawn from the milecastles and their
gateways dismantled, the turrets fell into disuse.   But
apparently the large forts kept a fighting garrison, though
obviously detachments of men must have been withdrawn
from them to man the forts of the Antonine Wall.   Certain
it is that at this period causeways were made across the
Vallum giving unimpeded comings and goings at many
points, as if it were no longer of any significance.   It was
almost as if, in Britain at any rate, it was supposed that a

permanent peace had descended upon the province, and military stations south of the Antonine Wall were no longer of importance.

Nothing could have been farther from the truth.   In the year 155 came a rude awakening to grim realities.   In that year there flared up what was destined to be the last serious revolt of the Brigantes.   Troops guarding the Antonine Wall were probably recalled to deal with it, and the completion of the conquest of the Lowlands became an impossibility.   Eventually the Brigantes were quelled and their lands were even more heavily garrisoned than before, as far south as modern Derbyshire; and subsequently that warlike race gave no further trouble.   The north was never to be so deeply and extensively romanized as the south, however.   It remained to the end a military area, while the south— except in later years, and then only in south-eastern coastal areas—was void of garrisons, military stations and campaigning grounds.   The 'villa economy' of peaceful existence which became prevalent in the south did not spread to the north.   But a few urban communities grew up and managed to flourish in the north.   There was, for instance, the civil settlement outside the walls of the legionary fortress of the Sixth Legion at Eboracum; there was the little town of Isurium (Aldborough), fragments of whose walls and mosaic pavements may still be seen; and there was Corstopitum. Corstopitum's fortunes ebbed and flowed with those of Hadrian's Wall.   It flourished till the evacuation of the Wall towards the end of the fourth century; it either decayed away or was destroyed when the withdrawal of the Wall's protection laid it wide open and defenceless under the attacks of the old enemy, the Caledonians of the far north. But that lay a long time ahead; and much was to happen in Britain before that day came.

VIII · TOWN AND COUNTRY LIFE

By now the Romans had been over a hundred years in
Britain; and perhaps this is a convenient point at which
to pause for a while and consider the life of the people
in town and country while the events we have been describing were taking place.

An eighteenth-century enquirer into those times would
more readily have pictured the aspect of Britain during the
early centuries of our era than we are able to do today. For
in the last one hundred and fifty years our island has become
predominantly industrial: a land of sprawling, overcrowded
towns, dense populations, huge industrial installations, and
a countryside scarred and marred by motor-traffic, nuclear
power stations, steel-works and opencast mining. We are
apt to forget that up to the end of the eighteenth century
England was a pastoral and agricultural country, untouched
by industrialism. And it was essentially the same in
Roman times, a land of country houses in the midst of farms,
where towns existed only as market-centres for the selling of
the surplus produce of the farms and the supplying of such
luxuries as those mainly self-supporting entities could not
provide for themselves, or as centres of administration for the
rural areas around them—country towns, as we should call
them nowadays, though on a smaller scale than those of the
present age.

The governor, Ostorius Scapula, is credited, as we have
said, with building the first Roman-type town in Britain—at
Camulodunum, for his legionary veterans. This was a *colonia*.
There were three other *coloniae*—Lincoln, Gloucester and
York. Though such towns were inhabited by Britons as
well as by veteran soldiers, they were at first predominantly
Roman; so much so in the case of Scapula's Camulodunum
that it roused fires of resentment in the breasts of the Iceni,
and contributed to Boudicca's revolt in 61, as we have seen.
The town was speedily rebuilt after the Boudiccan disaster;

E

but it seems soon to have happened that Londinium, owing
to its superior geographical situation, began to take precedence over the original capital of the province—if we may
use that term for something that did not exist in Roman
times in the sense in which we use it now.   Londinium
grew to be the pre-eminent centre of trade, the gathering-
place of all the wealthy merchants; and very early it
became the centre for the financial administration of the
province and the seat of the procurator as well.   In later
times its importance in the government of Britain grew
greater still.

The *coloniae* were very likely the earliest Roman-built
towns, and their military origin was obvious.   But in fact
military architects and engineers had a marked influence on
the lay-out of all government-sponsored towns, into whatever category they fell.   We have mentioned in dealing with
Agricola the other important category—the tribal or cantonal capitals.   It was part of Roman policy in Celtic lands
to make use of pre-existing native organization if this could
be so adapted as to conform to Roman usage; and to intro-
duce their ideas of civilization through the former Celtic-
speaking chieftains and the native notables and aristocratic
families.   These had held sway over the countryside around
their strongholds and over the dwellers and labourers therein, very much as eighteenth-century squires were to do in the
days to come.   Now they were enticed by the Romans into
towns founded upon the sites of Celtic market and tribal
centres, places sacred to tribal gods and their rites, or
formerly existing 'townships' of the Celtic kind, like Calleva
of the Belgic Atrebates.   We have seen how Agricola was
the first to encourage the building or romanized rebuilding
of such centres with the aid of his military engineers, who
would naturally plan them in the design of a Roman camp.
The chieftains and other notables were then honoured (in
earlier times they considered it an honour; it was only later
that they grew to hate it as an irksome and expensive duty)
by being appointed to administer the affairs of the town in
the town council or *ordo*.   The Britons who assumed office as
magistrates were awarded Roman citizenship *ex officio*—a
much coveted honour in the days before 212, when Roman

citizenship was granted outright to every freeborn individual within the Empire.

Of the hundred members of the *ordo* four magistrates were elected annually from among the British inhabitants of the town; two senior, who were justices and dealt with most civil and minor criminal cases; cases involving capital punishment had to be referred to the Roman governor or his deputy at the assize courts, and a junior pair concerned with such business as contracts and the repair of public buildings. The hundred members of the *ordo* were called decurions; the Quinquinnalis, which was appointed every five years, filled any vacancies by the appointment of suitable citizens for life. The chief responsibility of the decurions, besides the administration of the town, was the collection of the taxes in money or in kind for the Roman government. The taxes in kind, which were sent to specified depôts, were chiefly corn and leather to satisfy the needs of the army.

These councillors, all wealthy British landowners, would have their town house for the accommodation of themselves and their families when their duties demanded their presence in town. The rest of the time they would live on their country estates. (Once more we are reminded of the life of an eighteenth-century landowner.) Their town house would be a roomy, comfortable dwelling in the residential quarter of the town, generally a building on stone or brick foundations with half-timbering above, like a Tudor house, except that most Romano-British dwellings of the lordlier kind show no indubitable remains of staircases, and therefore seem to have had no upper storey. They did, however, have gardens, even in the towns. For the 'gentry' there were no terrace houses, there was no crowding. On the other hand the shopkeepers and artisans of the town would be housed in long, narrow buildings close together on either side of the main street: the shops on the ground floor, open in front for the display of wares in the later mediaeval fashion, with a room behind used for stores, and an upper storey where the shopkeeper or craftsman and his family lived, over his business premises.

The stereotyped plan of a Roman camp was a rectangle with a gate in each of its four sides and two roads leading to these gates crossing at right-angles in the middle of the camp; at their junction, right in the centre of the camp, was the *Principia*, the Headquarters building, and the barracks around would be set out on a grid pattern, with straight, parallel streets. The military mind which influenced the lay-out of the tribal capitals carried this plan over to them. There would be the grid pattern of streets and the main roads approaching the four gates, and where they crossed at right-angles, in the centre of the town, would be the civilian equivalent of the Headquarters building: the town hall with its forecourt or market-place—or in Roman parlance, the basilica and forum.

The public buildings of a Romano-British town were what especially distinguished it as being Roman, not Celtic. The forum and basilica were the chief of these, the forum being a rectangular court with (if the town could afford it) a monumental entrance in the middle of one side immediately facing the basilica across the paved court, which was a meeting place—originally a market-place—for all and sundry. Here you hailed your friends, talked over any news, and generally watched the world go by. Round three sides of the court there would be a colonnaded walk with administrative offices and shops. (We are only now beginning to return to the civilized idea of providing covered ways in which you may do your shopping out of the rain.) The basilica would usually take up the whole of the fourth side. (A solitary wall of such a basilica, preserved to a good height, still exists at Leicester.) The basilica, town hall, or hall of justice as you will, was an aisled building divided internally by pillars; it had an apsidal alcove at one or both ends. Here was a dais, here sat the chief officiating magistrate to deliver justice. It was the form of this basilica, so familiar throughout the Roman Empire, which was later adopted, in Britain as elsewhere in the West (*not* in the East, the Greek half of the Empire) for the services of the Christian Church.

No town which had any civic pride would have been without that peculiarly Roman institution, the *thermae*, or public bath-building. Here we must rid ourselves of the Victorian image of public baths—those dingy, white-tiled buildings smelling of steam to which, half a century ago, those

who had no bath-
rooms in their houses
crept shame-facedly,
in which they had a
hurried immersion in
a solitary cubicle and
from which they then
as hastily departed.
In Roman Britain, as
in the rest of the Em-
pire, very few town
houses had private
baths—one was ex-
pected to visit the *thermae* as a part of social
life. The poor, no
doubt, had no time
to linger in them,
though, like everyone
else, they visited them
daily; but those in
easier circumstances
would spend perhaps
a whole afternoon in
them, meeting their
friends, discussing the
affairs of the town, ex-
changing gossip and
scandal. The baths
could be, and often

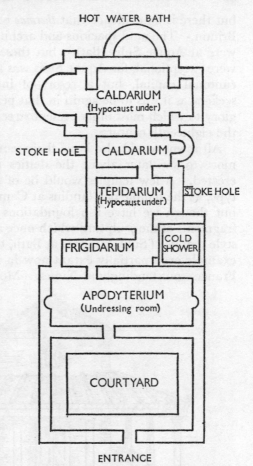

PLAN OF ROMAN BATHS AT SILCHESTER

were, buildings of great magnificence, with lounges, dressing-
rooms, a series of variously heated chambers through which
the bathers passed in turn, sweating profusely in the hottest
chamber—for the system was rather that of the Turkish bath
than the hot-water bath to which we are accustomed.
There would then be scraping and anointing by slaves, and
perhaps a plunge in the cold-water bath to close the pores.
Some *thermae* had swimming baths attached to them. In
Rome and other important cities of Italy there would be
gymnasia, lecture-halls and libraries attached to the *thermae*,

but there is no evidence that *thermae* on this scale existed in Britain. The most spacious and architecturally magnificent were at Aquae Sulis (Bath); but these were medicinal and were exceptional, for Aquae Sulis was neither a *colonia* nor a cantonal capital, but a resort of invalids and pleasure-seekers, as it was to be again in that period of its resurrected glory to which most of its present streets and houses belong, the eighteenth century.

All towns would also have their temples. We shall have more to say later about the deities to whom these were erected. A few temples would be of the familiar, classical type, as the temple of Claudius at Camulodunum had been, but though we have the foundations of that temple, and fragments of the sculpture which once adorned the classical-style temple of Sulis-Minerva at Bath, there is no upstanding example even partially extant now in Britain, as there is in France—outstandingly at Nîmes. Most temples in Britain,

PROBABLE APPEARANCE OF A ROMANO-CELTIC TEMPLE

however, would have been of the Celtic type: small, box-shaped buildings with a tiled roof and ambulatories surrounding them. These will be described in more detail in a later chapter.

Some towns would also boast theatres for dramatic shows —open to the sky, with a semi-circular auditorium rising steeply in tiers. These always *were* built on the classical Roman (not Greek) pattern. Or a town might have in addition to, or instead of, a theatre, an amphitheatre for chariot-racing or gladiatorial shows. They were ovoid, and resembled our modern sports arenas, the audience sitting all round the area where the contest was to take place; like the theatres, they were open to the sky. In Britain, again, there are no such splendid remains, as at Orange in Provence (the *provincia*), of a Roman-style theatre, or at Arles and Nîmes, of amphitheatres; but there are recognizable remains of a theatre at Verulamium (St. Albans) and the mound of the amphitheatre is traceable at Corinium (Cirencester) and Durnovaria (Dorchester in Dorset). Some massive stone-work of the buttresses of an apparently very large theatre was also found during the excavation of sites bombed in the Second World War in Canterbury (the Roman Durover-num), but this is no longer visible.

Some towns had inns for the general public—there was apparently one in Calleva; and all those towns, like Rochester in Kent or Kenchester in Herefordshire, which were situated on important roads, would have their *mansiones* for changing horses and the refreshment of imperial messengers.

Most towns from the second century onwards would be surrounded by walls, as they were to be again in the Middle Ages. Indeed, the still existing mediaeval walls of several towns—London and Canterbury, for instance—are demon-strably built upon the foundations of the original Roman ones. Where a Romano-British town has been deserted since Roman times, the original Roman walls sometimes remain, as at Calleva, where great stretches are obvious to the most untrained eye. But even in some places where a modern town has grown up in later centuries on top of the Romano-British one, considerable lengths of the Roman walls (usually, in this case, much patched in mediaeval times) may still be seen. An outstanding example is at Colchester, old Camulodunum; but London is not without its half-hidden remnants if you know where to look for them. And at Caerwent, the Venta Silurum of those trouble-makers in the days of Ostorius Scapula and Cerealis, the Silures, now only a village, but still inhabited, not only the east and south walls, the latter with its bastions, but also the north and south gates are plainly visible. And at Verulamium, beyond an upstanding stretch of much robbed wall, you may see a fine example of the town ditch, dating from the late second or early third century.

When we follow the circuit of these remaining walls, however, we are inevitably struck by one great difference between Romano-British and modern towns—the ancient ones are all, without exception, by modern standards very small.   We can see this clearly at Caistor-by-Norwich, which is now an abandoned site, never built on after Roman times.   The smallest towns of all were those fifty or so little ones in eastern and southern England and parts of the west, like Rochester in Kent and Kenchester mentioned above, which were a combination of pure market-centre and posting station, situated at the junction of highroads.

Outside the town walls, in great stretches all around, lay the countryside, far more afforested then than now, but especially in the southern half of Britain, rich with spreading farmlands, and in the midst of the farmlands, the homes, the 'manor houses' of the well-to-do farmers and landowners: the so-called 'Roman villas'.   The term is misleading.   In the first place they were not Roman in the sense that they belonged to Romans; nor were they, at any rate after the first century, built by Romans; nor were they even copies of the houses built in those centuries in classical Mediterranean lands.   In the second place they can only be thought of as 'villas' if we use that Latin word strictly in its Latin sense of 'farm-house' or 'manor house'.

They were dwellings of varying sizes built in a style better suited to a cold and often sunless northern land than was necessary in Italy; and though Roman building methods were used in their construction it was Roman-taught British or Gallic workmen who used them, and Britons who lived in them—such Britons as would have been called 'lords of the manor' in centuries long after the Romans had gone.   Like manor houses of those later centuries they were self-supporting, living off the produce of the land around them, getting from the nearest town only such luxury articles as could not be produced at home.   Roman standards of living were adopted in them—to such a degree they were 'Roman'; their British owners spoke Latin as well as Celtic, and as time went

on adopted Roman dress, manners and customs; but in only
a few instances were the dwellers in these 'villas' real
Romans. A Roman official does indeed seem to have lived
for part of the time at Lullingstone, in Kent; and at Folkestone it has been assumed that some naval officer dwelt in
the villa discovered there in the nineteen-twenties but since
covered-in—though even he was probably not a Roman, but
an official of provincial origin.

In the days between Julius Caesar's reconnaissances and
the conquest of the land by the legions of Claudius, 'villas'
had already appeared sparsely in south-east Britain, inspired
not directly by the Romans, but by the Romano-Gallic style
of building familiar to the south-east owing to frequent
intercourse between that area of Britain and romanized Gaul.
But these non-Celtic, Gallo-Roman houses were all small and
unpretentious. Afterwards, when influence and guidance
in building technique came from the Romans in Britain
themselves, some of the houses erected in the southern half
of the island grew to vast proportions, like the one unearthed
last century at Bignor in Sussex. In this connection, however, it should be remembered, as we have said before, that
the majority of these romanized dwellings apparently had
no upper storeys, so that, all the accommodation being on the
ground floor, they appear now to be more spacious than they
actually were.

There are two main types of villa: the corridor (the earlier)
and the courtyard (a later development). The corridor
houses had a range of rooms, ideally facing south, with a
slight projecting wing at each end. In front of this main
range, between the two wings, was a low wall of stone or
brick upon which stood dwarf columns occasionally of
timber, more often of stone, supporting a pentice roof of
tiles; this formed a covered way on to which the main rooms
opened, and in the middle was a porch, with steps down from
the colonnade to the open ground in front. Roman houses
had windows filled with translucent bluish-green glass; these
were set high up in the room so as to look out above the
pentice roof in the manner of a clerestory in an aisled church.
At the rear of the house there might be another corridor.
Earlier villas, and the smaller ones of later times, had no

special bath-buildings; but most of the later villas had them, often (as at Bignor) separated from the main part of the house to guard against the danger of fire. The villas, like the grander town houses, were built on stone foundations—the only part of them, as a general rule, which we now see—with a timber-framed structure above, and a roof of red tiles overlapping in the Roman manner, or if the locality provided them, of flat stone slabs, generally lozenge-shaped. Thus, as far as we can tell, a Romano-British house of the better type would not have been in the least like a pillared classical residence. It would, as we have said, have resembled rather an English Tudor house. Externally, like most Roman buildings both public and private, it would have been brightly painted.

POSSIBLE APPEARANCE OF A ROMANO-BRITISH VILLA

A resident staff of farm-labourers, slaves and free men, would live close by in barn-like buildings ranged along the sides of the open ground in front of the villa. These buildings would be divided into 'nave' and 'aisles' by timber columns, and would have resembled those mediaeval barns we may still see here and there in the countryside. In the 'nave' would be kept the stores and farm tools together with livestock; in the 'aisles' the labourers would live and sleep. The domestic servants, practically all slaves, would have their quarters in a certain part of the house set aside for them.

As time went on the two projecting wings of these villas tended to lengthen, and as they did so an enclosing wall with an entrance-gate was built to join their ends. Thus was formed a courtyard villa. The lengthened wings would now contain stabling, wagon-stands, workshops, and in many cases all the impedimenta of a farm would clutter the courtyard. But in the wealthier houses it was considered undesirable to look out from the main reception rooms on to such a utilitarian rather than beautiful medley, so all this was relegated to further enclosures outside the wall of the courtyard, and the courtyard itself would become a garden for the pleasure of the villa's owners, with flowers and paths, pools perhaps, and fountains.

The main room of the house, usually facing the porch in the colonnade, was the *triclinium*, or dining-room, and this was the most romanized room in the house after the Britons adopted the Roman custom of reclining on couches at meals. It was this room above all the others which was likely to be made splendid with a tessellated pavement—a 'mosaic' rectangle which today is always the most spectacular part of an excavated Roman villa, and the scattered tesserae of which often proclaim that a Roman villa is under the earth close by. Of course, in the richer houses tessellated pavements do occur in more rooms than one, and sometimes even in corridors—there is an example at Canterbury. They were the 'carpets' of antiquity, albeit less suited than carpets to our colder climate, and they were laid wherever we should lay carpets, if the owner of the house could afford them, for the making and laying of a mosaic floor was an expensive business, and most people had to be sparing in their use of this embellishment, and use the cheaper *opus signinum*— a cement made of lime and small fragments of broken brick rubbed down to a smooth surface and polished.

Some of these pavements remain in their original positions, exactly where the craftsmen of fifteen centuries ago placed them—*in situ*, as we say. Many more have been taken up in recent times and are on view in various museums up and down the country—in the museum at Dorchester in Dorset they are actually serving their original function of being walked on by visitors. Verulamium prefers to set its specimens upright against the wall—an unnatural position; but if you want to see a pavement at Verulamium as the Romano-Britons saw it you have only to walk across the grass of the park and you may do so, for the pavement there is *in situ*, with a few courses of its villa's walls still surrounding it.   Some of the best *in situ* mosaics, however, are at Lullingstone in Kent, Chedworth in Gloucestershire, Bignor in Sussex and Brading in the Isle of Wight.   A very fine museum-piece is the 'Christian' mosaic from Hinton St. Mary, Dorset, now displayed prominently in the British Museum; but no mosaic pavement that has been lifted out of its original environment can ever stir in us quite the same feelings as one *in situ* does.

The Roman mosaic which the Britons adopted, unlike the Byzantine, which was formed of coloured glass, or of glass over gold foil, was made of cubes of pottery or stone set in a bed of cement, and in Britain it is found only in floors. (Byzantine mosaics more commonly decorate walls or vaulted roofs.)

White cubes were made from chalk, red from brick or tiles, or Samian ware, buff from sandstone, blue from slate, black and dark grey from slate and limestone and yellow from gravel.   These are the colours which occur most frequently, though others are occasionally found.   Presumably the cheapest type of mosaic pavement to design and lay, as requiring a little less skill—it is the most common, anyway—was composed of conventional and geometric designs.   Sets of panels divided by bands of guilloche (that is, double or triple plaits of intertwisted ribbon design) or more rarely, the Greek key-pattern, have a central decoration in them of eight-pointed stars, rosettes or ingenious perspectives producing optical illusions like Bignor's 'conical boxes'.   Or borders carry tendrils ending in heart-shaped leaves twining out of two-handled, urn-like vases.   There are also 'labyrinth' or maze designs around a central panel containing perhaps a sea-god's horned head or a gawky lion devouring a stag, all edged with the inevitable guilloche; circles and squares and lozenges are superimposed upon one another.   Only occasionally do we shake off the ubiquitous guilloche, get away from the leaf-hearts and the two-handled

vases, and find something more original in the way of conventional design: the 'rising sun'—or, as some will have it,
the 'scallop shell'—at Verulamium, for instance, bordered
with an attractive wave-crest pattern. But of course the
most interesting and more uncommon mosaic pavements,
because possibly the more expensive (though even so not
always very expertly executed) are those which show figure
subjects.

Among a variety of these the most frequently found are the
busts representing the Seasons, in medallions which con-
veniently fill the corners of rectangular pavements: Spring,
represented as a young boy or girl with a bird on his or her
shoulder, Summer with scarlet poppies in her hair, Autumn
garlanded with fruit or ripe corn, and the mournful, hooded
head of Winter with a leafless branch across her shoulder.
The central subjects to which these medallions may be the
outer adornments are many, but much repetition occurs.
Hunting scenes with dogs chasing hares or stags, or lions and
leopards pursuing their prey were popular; so were Greek
legends. We see Actaeon transformed into a stag being
torn by his own hounds, and Cyparissus with the beloved
stag which he accidentally slew (occurring once only, it
seems, at Leicester); Daphne followed by Apollo, Ganymede
borne aloft by Jove's eagle to be cupbearer to the gods,
Orpheus charming the beasts and birds with his music (this
subject, occurring often, may have had some religious
significance), Perseus and Andromeda, Bellerophon spearing
the Chimaera and the Rape of Europa. More rarely, as far
as we know, for innumerable pavements must have been
destroyed long ago, or else are lying buried under the earth,
literature supplied subjects, and we find scenes from the
Aeneid in a mosaic pavement from Low Ham, in Somerset
(now in the Taunton Museum). Occasionally the meaning
of the subject represented is now lost to us. What, for
instance, is the man with a cock's head and claws and spurs
doing as he approaches a ladder leaning against a house,
while two winged griffins hover near by? This is in the villa
at Brading, Isle of Wight. But most of the Brading mosaics
are unusual, and were evidently specially commissioned for
some reason by a wealthy patron who did not want anything

from stock patterns—just as nowadays those who have
sufficient money may have their curtains woven for them
and their wallpapers designed to their individual fancy,
while the rest of us have to be satisfied with what is in the
pattern-book.   It is at Brading that the less common legend
of Ceres giving seed to Triptolemus appears, and Hercules
presenting the Amazonian axe to Omphale, Queen of Lydia;
and it is there that we may see the most unusual subject of
the astrologer (perhaps Hipparchus, the inventor of instru-
ments to mark the magnitude and situation of each star, and
the relationship of the stars to the destinies of man) pointing
with a wand to a sphere on a tripod, above which is a pillar
surmounted by a sundial.

Winged cupids in the guise of gladiators fight their battles,
or are armed for the fray in a long horizontal panel at
Bignor; Tritons and mermaids play and gambol at Brading;
at Cirencester Silenus is represented as a jolly old demi-god
riding backwards on an ass, holding a wine-cup in one hand
and a bridle in the other.   For the Seasons in corner medallions are sometimes substituted busts of the Four Winds.
The head of Venus, flanked by long-tailed peacocks, appears
in a medallion at Bignor above the doings of the cupids who
are pretending to be gladiators.   More often, however, it is
Medusa's head we see, the snakes writhing out of it like
quivering rays of light from a pictured sun.   But the rarest
bust of all (again, as far as we know) is that in a medallion
among the hunting scenes of the fine Hinton St. Mary pavement now in the British Museum, which has been mentioned
above: a head which is arguably, though not certainly, that of
Christ, for it is depicted in front of the Chi-Rho (a monogram
formed from the initial letters in Greek of Christ's name—a
Christian symbol).   The chief objection to this indenti-
fication of the bust is that it is doubtful whether a representation of the head of Christ would be placed in a position where
it would inevitably be constantly trodden underfoot.

This, of course, is by no means a complete catalogue of all
the subjects found in such tessellated pavements which have
been brought to light in our country, but it is enough to show
that amongst much stereotyping there was also a fair amount
of variety, even in the fraction which has been recovered

from an original output which must have been far larger.

The Romans did not, as we do, paste ornamental papers nor hang framed canvases on their walls; they plastered and painted them. Since all these walls have long since fallen, and painted plaster is in any case a perishable material, it is difficult for us to assess the original effect of this decoration from the faded fragments which we find and laboriously try to piece together. Whether there were any wall-paintings in Britain to equal those which have been discovered almost intact in Pompeii, Herculaneum, Boscoreale and Stabiae we are not in a position to know; but it is unlikely, since wall-paintings could not be imported, and though the painters might have been, their work would have been too expensive for most Romano-Britons; provincial artists probably produced all such paintings in Britain.

Many museums display fragments of painted wall-plaster from Romano-British buildings, most of them too small to give any adequate idea of their overall effect. On the whole, if we may justly judge by these extant fragments, it would seem that even in their pristine unfaded state the painted walls of Romano-British houses would not have appealed to modern taste. Sombre maroon backgrounds sprinkled with greyish-blue and white leaves and flowers; black, grey and off-white lines marking out maroon panels; dull reddish-brown enlivened with groups of thin orange stripes; dark ochre paintings of conventional plant-life on cream, green or olive with yellow outlinings—should we care to live nowadays with these around us, even if they were much brighter long ago? But we must remember that Romano-British cushions, tasselled pillows and curtains, and textiles to cover chairs and stools were made of red, gold and blue linen; wool embroidered in gaily coloured silks, and purple, scarlet and dark green draperies decked with stripes of red, yellow and purple covered bedsteads, while cloth-of-gold was by no means unknown. All the same, Lieutenant-Colonel Meates gives a horrifying description of decoration that was discovered in the corridor leading to the bath-house at the villa at Lullingstone, where there was, he says,[1] a line of white panels within deep red and purple painted 'pillars',

----

[1] G. W. Meates, *Lullingstone Roman Villa*, pp. 50–51.

the surface of which was covered with half-finished purple circles, loops and curves of every sort, as if the artist had 'sat down before each panel and quickly, without any sort of plan, let himself go, twirling his brush of purple paint in a mad frenzy this way and that'. He wonders if this 'mad complexity of curvature' perhaps reflected a resurgence, very much debased, of Celtic taste.

Judging again from some of the painted plaster recovered at Lullingstone, we presume that slight attempts were sometimes made to follow the Roman fashion for perspective views; for rectangular panels in a rich, deep red have been pieced together there, bounded by thin white and dark blue lines, the panels being drawn in perspective; and what is called by the excavators of the villa the 'Deep Room' had a dado all round it—dados were apparently popular in room decoration—consisting of alternate squares and lozenges supporting very large panels outlined in red, orange and green, also with a suggestion of perspective. It was a common Roman practice in earlier times to have pictures of gardens, groves, romantic-looking houses and temples embowered in trees painted in such panels, so that one seemed to be looking through a window at these scenes, but no evidence of such pictures has as yet been found in Britain.

Lullingstone, probably owing to the sloping ground on which the villa is built, had the rare feature of an upper storey, and consequently staircases; and traces have been found of the painted decoration once on the wall beside one of these. It was a red painted balustrade with a red skirting below, both rising along the wall at the same angle as the stairs; between them was a painted latticework. Such information really makes us see again as homes those Romano-British dwellings which sank into the earth so long ago.

But we have the evidence of many surviving fragments to show that there were other types of wall-painting besides these geometric and conventional designs. We can see pieces of maroon-coloured plaster with plant decoration in natural colours, as if a garden were represented on them. We can also see a pink and dark blue fish swimming in pale blue water which seems to have belonged to the Lullingstone bath-house; or the sizable panel, pieced together from fragments, of the bird and floral scroll which once was somebody's pride and joy in Verulamium. Birds and natural plant-life are always well delineated, and that is more than can be said for the human beings. And that these were represented we have incontrovertible proof. In the Newport Museum in Wales, which displays pieces of plaster from Venta Silurum (Caerwent) there is part of a face painted on one fragment, belonging to someone in a blue and green dress; the hand holding a flower on another fragment probably belongs to this same lady. At Letocetum (Wall—a Roman military station near what is now Lichfield, in Staffordshire) a woman's painted eyes, arched eyebrows and nose appears among conventional four-petalled flowers, coloured brown, with pale green leaves, in circles. And in the Duke of Northumberland's museum in Alnwick Castle there is depicted on a chunk of wallplaster a man in a white toga holding a staff; a seated figure, garlanded and dressed in blue and yellow, holding a torch; and a striding figure in a yellow dress holding on to a piece of green drapery. All of these are on a grey background—which may, of course, have faded from an original more cheerful blue.

But by far the most interesting figural wall-paintings come again from Lullingstone. There were two painted areas with which we are concerned in this connection. The earlier —earlier by perhaps two centuries—is in the 'Deep Room' mentioned above. This room was obviously once a Nymphaeum, or shrine of Water Nymphs, often an accompaniment of villas near rivers, streams or springs.[1] This painting still dimly exists, and after restoration is now on public view. Here in the 'Deep Room', in one of the earlier places of habitation of the villa, was a small, second-century well, and near it was a round-headed niche. It is in this niche that the painting occurs.

It shows two (there were originally three) water nymphs (such sprites usually go in threes.) One is standing, and has water spurting from her breasts; her head, which is still clearly visible, has leaves and an aureole around it. She

---

[1] Lullingstone is on the bank of the river Darent which now, however, has receded some way from the villa.

FRESCO OF WATER NYMPHS AT THE VILLA AT LULLINGSTONE

holds a frond in her hand.   On her right is a seated nymph
whose face is now indistinguishable; she wears a blue robe
falling over her knees and holds a water-pot turned upside-
down in her right hand.   Of the third nymph not much can
be made out today.   This painting is classical in feeling,
and the subdued colours remind one of paintings in the overwhelmed cities at the base of Vesuvius; but as we have said,
Lullingstone villa is one of the few that really does appear to
have been inhabited, for a time at least, by a Roman official
and his truly Roman family, and his Mediterranean taste is
no doubt reflected in this painting.

The other wall-painting, found in thousands of fallen fragments among the débris in this same 'Deep Room', into which the walls had collapsed in the fire which finally destroyed the villa, probably at the end of the fourth century or beginning of the fifth, without doubt came from the upper room which in later days had been built over the 'Deep Room', sealing it off. The staircase with the red banister and skirting and the latticework between had led up to this room; and inside the door, on its west wall, above a flowered dado, were painted, in the last decades of the villa's life, alternate red and blue columns, and between each pair an *orant*—that is, a figure with head raised and arms out-stretched in the classical attitude of prayer. There is a child, a young boy, a man, a confused jumble of someone not perfectly distinguishable, a lady, and a figure seated in a magisterial chair. The young boy is particularly clear. He stands in front of a curtain (this would seem to signify that he has died, and belongs to the spirit world beyond the grave) and he looks out at us with big, sorrowful and haunt-ing eyes. As evidence came to light from other fragments of wall-plaster that there had been painted on the south wall close by a Chi-Rho symbol surrounded by a wreath, and that another had existed on the wall of the vestibule at the head of the stairs, it is conjectured that all this was the decoration of a Christian 'House Church', of the kind found at Dura-Europos in North Syria. Whether any other such House Churches existed in Britain we do not as yet know.

It will be understood that in dealing with both mosaics and wall-paintings we have necessarily wandered far beyond the bounds of the second century, where we left our account of the history of Roman Britain. Signs of Christianity in Britain, like these at Lullingstone, are all late—we cannot be certain of any in this country ante-dating the fourth century.

It has taken us fifteen hundred years to re-discover one amenity which the Romano-Britons took for granted in even the smallest of their villas—an amenity introduced to them, it goes without saying, by the Romans, who had no mind to endure with our resignation the coldness of a house in a British winter and spring. They soon enlightened the Britons on the subject of central heating. Underneath the floors of a house they built hypocausts—a series of brick or stone dwarf pillars supporting the floors, round which circulated air heated from a furnace at the entrance to the hypocaust. This hot air found its way into box-flues made of tiles and inserted in the walls of the room or rooms above. It was a system similar to that which had in warmer climes heated bath-buildings. Of course, one hypocaust would heat only rooms adjacent to it; other hypocausts had to be built under rooms requiring to be heated in farther wings of the house. In exceptionally cold weather, where we should supplement our central heating with electric fires, the Romano-Britons used portable braziers burning charcoal.

Although we should consider these villas sparsely furnished, such furniture as there was, even to the kitchen utensils, was elegant and handsome. It consisted of bronze-mounted wooden chests, couches of maplewood, beech, willow or oak, armchairs of 'scissor' style, folding stools of iron with plaited leather seats and wickerwork chairs very like the 'basket' chairs fashionable not so many years ago; round tables on

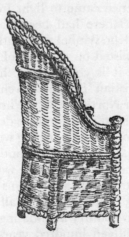

ROMAN BASKET CHAIR

three curved legs with animal heads of bronze at the top and ending in leonine claw feet, divan-like bedsteads of veneered woods, bronze tripods for decorative oil lamps and marble benches for the bath-building. All these were made bright, as we have said, by plentiful cushions, hangings, draperies,

coverlets and pillows.   Life in such houses so furnished must
have been very pleasant for the well-to-do Britons, the
prosperous farmer or tribal landowner, guarded from foes
by the ever-present Roman army, grumbling at heavy taxation, no doubt, but enjoying his comfortable centrally-
heated home with its pleasant views over the countryside, his
private baths, and labour for both house and farm, servile or
free, easy to come by.   We speak here, let it be understood,
of the days of the third and early fourth centuries.

For the peasants, however, life was not very different from
what it had always been in the days of old, when the chieftain
had lived in comparative squalor in his hill-top dun.   For
this part of the population was hardly, if at all, touched by
romanization.   Such inhabitants of the rural areas of the
land did not learn to speak Latin, as even the lower classes
in the towns did—they wrote it, too—nor did they adopt
Roman dress and manners and customs.   They continued
to live in villages of beehive-shaped, thatched huts dotted
about an area of two or three acres without any pretence of
regularity, surrounded by a bank so slight as now, after the
passage of fifteen hundred years, to be hardly discernible, and
a ditch beyond it.   The group of stone houses within a wall
of the same material at Din Lligwy in Anglesey—two houses
circular, the rest rectangular—was probably the stronghold
of pre-Roman and later chieftains, which existed right into
the fourth century; but the array of circular stone huts on
the lower slopes of Holyhead Mountain, where you may still
see the central hearth-stones in their places and the gaps for
the doorways, belong to the common people, the native
Celtic population untouched by Roman civilization and
living thus, in this remote spot, until the disastrous Irish
raids began in the fourth century.

But in the dry chalklands in the southern mainland of
Britain the huts would be of more perishable materials, and
sunk in the ground, so that you would step down from the
entrance into the single living-room, its floor of stamped
earth, its walls of wattle and daub; there would probably
have been no windows.   Such a village, existing at the
present day as a series of circular depressions in the grass, lay
below the ramparts of the stronghold on Eggardon Hill in

Dorset. In pre-Roman days the peasants inhabiting them would have driven their livestock, at signs of danger, behind the ramparts of this 'dun', the home of the local chieftain; the only difference in Roman times would have been the lack of necessity, at any rate in the southern half of Britain, to do this, for the occupation of the land by the Romans had ended the endemic inter-tribal warfare that had harassed the peasants in the years gone by.

In some peasants' houses excavation has discovered what appear to have been underground heating-chambers, and this has led to the belief that some of the peasants were in fact sufficiently romanized to understand and build hypocausts. But it is now generally agreed that such underground heating systems were only ovens for drying or parching corn.

Only occasionally do a few of the better huts show traces of painted plaster on their interior walls. In such huts Roman coins have also been found—the poorer peasants probably had no need to use money at all—and pottery of Roman type and minor specimens of jewellery of Roman manufacture.

One area of Britain—to this day unique—demands special mention: East Anglia and the easterly parts of Lincolnshire. Across this water-logged countryside the Romans cut canals to act as catchwaters and to link up with minor cuts which drained the Fens. The canals, in conjunction with natural waters, were also designed to facilitate transport. They linked Fenland with the river Witham in Lincolnshire, and as this was linked with the Trent by the Roman-made Foss Dyke, the Ouse and the Humber were attainable all the way by inland waters. It was indeed possible in Roman times to go by water from the Fens as far as York; and when we remember that there was a legionary fortress at York we can understand the value of these waterways for the transport of East Anglian produce—grain chiefly—to the military. The whole system was allowed to fall out of use after the departure of the Romans, and the Fens reverted to water-logged wasteland until the seventeenth century, when Dutchmen were brought in to do again what the Romans had done centuries before. Some of the Roman canals are still visible as shallow grooves between low flanking banks.

Britain in those days was not exclusively agricultural. The Romans exploited the mineral resources of the land. Although the ancient tin trade seems to have waned during the Occupation there were, in the Mendips and Derbyshire among other places, important lead mines (lead was used in the ancient world in the production of silver). There was even one gold mine in Carmarthenshire. Iron was also mined, especially in the Sussex Weald and the Forest of Dean, and there is evidence of limited coal-mining. Most of the mines were State property, and were worked by slaves or criminals supervised by soldiers.

One of the commonest industries, for its products were in perpetual demand, was coarse and fine pottery-making. Traces of pottery kilns of the Romano-British period are found in many places, but the most important centre of fine pottery making was at the kilns at Castor, near Peterborough in Northamptonshire; its kilns extended for miles along the banks of the river Nene. This blackish-brown *en barbotine* ware will be described more fully in a later chapter. Camulodunum (Colchester) produced from its own kilns similar pottery. Another, but shorter-lived centre lay in the New Forest area; its wares seem to have circulated in the south only.

We must not think of Britain during the Roman occupation as a mirror reflecting classical Rome. From the aristocracy to the artisans there was always, in all the Britons, the still-living Celt mingling with the superimposed Roman, producing something which, while it was not what it had been before the Romans came, was certainly not the culture of the classical lands round the Mediterranean. Indeed, even the aristocratic descendants of the former Celtic chieftains, now numbered amongst Roman citizens, did not really understand the culture of Cicero, Augustus, or Pliny. It was the romanization widespread throughout Gaul, so much nearer to them both geographically and ethnically, that they actually adopted. Superficially they might look and sound like the Romans of Rome, speaking Latin as they paraded the streets in their togas; superficially their way of life might resemble the Roman way, with its colonnaded town market-places, its basilicas and thermae and theatres and amphitheatres open to the sky, its altars of Roman form and monumental inscriptions in the unsurpassed Roman lettering; but in reality the Celt still lived and moved and had his being underneath, peeping out here and there in many small ways: love of the countryside in preference to the town, an adherence to his own native gods, and an upsurge every now and then of the dynamic Celtic artistry which was crushed down beneath the weight of Roman fashions but never killed.   We shall have more to say about this last in a later chapter.

IX · NOTES ON THE ROMAN ARMY IN BRITAIN

Before we go on with a history in which the army plays so large a part we should understand the nature of that army as far as it concerns Britain.

Three legions, as we have seen, remained on permanent guard in Britain: the Second at Isca (Caerleon), the Twentieth at Deva (Chester), and the Sixth (after the disappearance of the Ninth in some unrecorded disaster in Yorkshire) at Eboracum (York). These legions were field armies of regular, professional soldiers, quartered some way back from the actual frontiers of the province in large, permanent, stone-walled fortresses; the Second guarded the Bristol Channel, and was ready to move forward into the Welsh mountains in case of trouble; the Twentieth kept an eye on North Wales and the western Pennines in that troublesome area, Brigantia—later it became necessary for it also to watch the Irish Sea—and the Sixth controlled the eastern Pennines and was expected to reinforce the line of Hadrian's Wall (or at one period the Antonine Wall) if it became necessary. Each legion was commanded by a *legatus*, the emperor's representative sent out from Rome. We have seen how Agricola was thus sent to command the Twentieth Legion in A.D. 71.

Ideally there were 6,000 fighting men in a legion, divided into ten cohorts which were each sub-divided into six centuries. Originally every legionary, who was always an infantryman, had to be a Roman citizen; but this qualification meant little after the Emperor Caracalla at the beginning of the third century (212) granted Roman citizenship to every free-born person in the Empire. In any case, in imperial times soldiers were not so easily come by that such a limitation could be adhered to; we find that even as early as the second century Britons were becoming legionaries—in the legions stationed in Britain—as well as auxiliaries. Nor had there ever been any limitation on promotion. A

legionary of ability, if he wished, could rise from the ranks
through a series of grades to become, eventually, a centurion.

The centurions, the commanders of the centuries, were the
backbone of the Roman army. That army was famed far
and wide, admired by friends and feared by foes, for its
strict discipline, its drilled efficiency, its training; and it was
the centurions who were responsible for its drill and training,
and who enforced discipline. In times of battle they also
commanded and led their century of 100 men in the attack.
The most able of them might rise further, and become
prefects or tribunes, who commanded the auxiliaries.

The cohorts of auxiliaries, commanded by prefects (*prae-
fecti*), were not, at this time, parts of the legion. They were
the provincials fighting in their native garb and with their
native weapons on the frontiers of the Empire. They
were considered irregular troops, without the status of the
legionaries. They served for a term of twenty-five years
(the legionary's was twenty) and their pay was less; and as
they were stationed on the frontiers they often bore the brunt
of any enemy attack. They were quartered in small forts
along the line of the frontier; in Britain we find them for
a while on the Antonine Wall, and for over three centuries on
the Wall of Hadrian.

These auxiliaries had in earlier days been recruited from
among newly conquered tribes, and they kept the name of
their tribe, and were referred to as the 'first cohort of
Batavians', or the 'second cohort of Thracians', or if they
were cavalry units, the 'first *ala* of Asturians', and so on. It
was not the normal rule, however, for them to serve in their
native territory, possibly owing to the encouragement that
might have given for mutiny and armed revolt against the
Romans. They were sent to another part of the Empire
altogether. So we find, garrisoning the forts along Hadrian's
Wall, Asturians from Spain, Tungrians from what is now
Belgium, Thracians, Sarmatians, Batavians, Dalmatians and
others, while levies raised in Britain might be found as far off
as the frontier-line along the Danube. But as the auxiliaries
settled down on some frontier—for instance, in Britain—men
to fill gaps in a unit caused by death or retirement tended to
be recruited not from the original foreign tribe which had

given its name to the cohort, but from the local population. Furthermore the auxiliaries often married local women (until the end of the third century serving soldiers were not allowed to marry, but any liaisons they made were officially recognized as legal marriages on their retirement, and the children of the union were considered legitimate); sons frequently followed the profession of their fathers, and after a time a cohort or *ala* of auxiliaries bearing the name of some foreign tribe would be likely to contain many native-born soldiers. At the end there would probably be more British cavalrymen in the first *ala* of Asturians than Spaniards, and most of the infantrymen in the second cohort of Thracians would be Brigantes.

All these soldiers, legionaries and auxiliaries alike, spoke Latin. They had to, for it was the language of command. But we should be mistaken if we thought of it as Ciceronian Latin. 'Army Latin' would be a better name for it, and the modern languages derived from it, French, Spanish, Italian and Rumanian, occasionally give us glimpses of its deviations from the classical. Let two examples illustrate the point. When the army referred to somebody's head, it does not seem to have used the classical word *caput*, but *testa*, meaning a tile or potsherd, later a skull. This was adopted by the Gauls as the only word for the object, and it ended up as *tête*. Also, a horse was not *equus* to the army, but *caballus*, a rather derogatory word for the animal, becoming through Gaulish, the normal French *cheval*.

A legionary had to be able to march twenty miles in five hours, carrying all his kit, which included, besides three days' rations and his mess-tin, a saw, an axe, an entrenching tool, and a wicker basket for the earth he threw up when digging the proscribed ditch around the night's camp; for even when it stayed only one night in a spot the Roman army always measured out and fortified an entrenched camp. The Roman soldier also had to be a regular commando, able to scale barriers, vault fences, leap across ditches and swim rivers and straits—we remember how Agricola required this of his troops when he crossed to Anglesey—and to take part in the rapid erection of temporary camps and fortifications. They were also trained to be masons capable of building a stone wall; for it was the legions, as we remarked before, not slaves, who raised Hadrian's Wall. But there were also, attached to every legion, specialist engineers, surveyors and sappers; while ordinary soldiers might, if they chose, specialize as signallers, armourers, medical orderlies, clerks and accountants. A legion was a self-contained unit and could do everything for itself.

The auxiliaries, as has been said, used their own native weapons: slings, bows and arrows, special types of sword or spear or javelin; but the legionaries' weapons were the *pilum*, the six-foot-long lance, and the short stabbing (not slashing) sword, and the dagger. Their uniform and defensive armour is familiar to all of us from numerous pictures; there is an excellent life-size model of a fully armed legionary in the Grosvenor Museum at Chester.

Roman artillery, having no explosive power like modern guns was not, of course, as powerful as even that of the pre-nuclear age. But ancient accounts are quite positive about its devastating destructive power. Normally artillery was employed only in sieges. The *catapultae* projected missiles on the cross-bow principle in a horizontal direction, their range being about 358 yards, the *ballistae* shot stones (later bolts or 'arrows') at an angle of 50 degrees with a range of 295 to 503 yards. These, while not explosive, came with impetus enough to smash a thick stone wall. One of the bolts from a *ballista*, shot, as we mentioned earlier, from Vespasian's artillery at the east gate of Maiden Castle, lodged in the spine of one of the defenders and broke his back. The *catapultae* disappear in the fourth century, and a new piece of heavy artillery was introduced alongside the *ballista*, called an *onager*. This was a kind of gigantic sling used for hurling heavy stones like Tudor 'cannon' balls.

The great fortresses at Caerleon, Chester and York were of some forty acres in extent—larger than many a Romano-British town. York and Chester have been so built over from the Middle Ages onwards that it is only in scattered cellars and under dug-up streets that we can come upon fragments of the fortress originally built on the site of the city, except for upstanding, broken stretches of its walls; and though Caerleon is today not much more than a village its houses cover a good proportion of the ancient fort, leaving only a comparatively small area open for excavation: the area of the streets of barrack-blocks. But the auxiliaries' forts, especially those on the line of Hadrian's Wall, were replicas on a smaller scale of the great legionary fortresses. From them, therefore, we may get some idea of what the legionary fortresses were like—above all from Vercovicium (Housesteads) and Cilurnum (Chesters), which have never been overwhelmed by later towns or villages, and have been excavated, Housesteads almost completely, Cilurnum in part —or rather, only certain parts have been left open to our view.

These two most fully excavated forts on the Wall illustrate two complementary functions of the auxiliary frontier army. Vercovicium on the bleak heights of the crags was garrisoned by an infantry cohort; Cilurnum, far more pleasantly situated in the valley on the banks of the north Tyne, where it guarded the bridge still traceable there, held a cavalry *ala*, originally of Asturians from Spain, where the best horsemen were said to be found. Here on the flat ground the cavalry could easily be deployed; the precipitous crags at Vercovicium were best protected by foot-soldiers.

All Roman forts were rectangular, rounded at the corners. Turrets were built on these corners, and at intervals along the high stone walls; a gate, usually double-portalled, with guardrooms, opened in each of the four walls. Outside was a deep ditch, surrounding the fort. Inside, in the centre, where the forum and basilica would be in a civilian town, was the most important building in the fort—the Headquarters (*principia*). Had we entered, fifteen or more centuries ago, through a gateway in the wall in front of it, having passed the sentry on guard, we should have found ourselves in a courtyard, and immediately ahead of us we should have seen the 'cross-hall'—a long building taking up the whole of one side of the courtyard. Entering it, we should at once have noticed a raised platform or tribunal at one end of it, and perhaps at the very moment of our arrival the commanding officer might have been standing or seated aloft on it, addressing his men, or hearing pleas, or pronouncing judgement on offenders. (The ruins at Vindolanda, a well-excavated fort

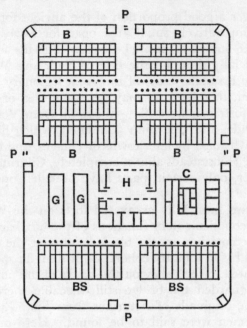

PLAN OF A ROMAN CAMP
B, Barracks; BS, Stables (if the unit were
a cavalry one); C, Commandant's House
(*Praetorium*); H, Headquarters Building
(*Principia*); G, Granaries; P, Gates (*Portae*)

about three miles south of Housesteads, which belonged to a
series planned by Agricola but renovated and rebuilt later,
are sufficiently complete to give a vivid idea of a cross-hall of
this kind, with its tribunal.)   Along the farther side of this
cross-hall we should have noticed the administrative quarters,
where all the clerking, book-keeping and quartermaster's
list-keeping was done; and our eyes would of course have
been drawn to the most sacred centre of the fort, the shrine
of the standards.   Underneath this would be the strong-
room, where the soldiers' pay and savings were banked.   At
Cilurnum on Hadrian's Wall we can in reality, not merely in
imagination, descend the stone steps of Roman days and
stand in the strong-room, and see its barrel-vaulting.

Near the Headquarters was the commanding officer's
house (*praetorium*) where, if he were married, his wife and

family could live with him: a comfortable, well-appointed house, very like a civilian one in town or country.   The rest of the fortress area was taken up with barrack blocks built, usually with pentice-roofed colonnades in front, along streets in a regular grid pattern; and against the fort walls would be stabling for cavalry units, workshops and sometimes cook-houses.   There would be a hospital somewhere in the fort, and—most important—granaries, raised from the ground on a series of little pillars resembling a hypocaust, for ventilation and to guard against rats.   Although the floors and upper walls of the granaries have vanished this ventilating system may be seen very clearly at Housesteads.   Outside the fort would be the soldier's bath-building.   An example has been excellently, one might almost say spectacularly, preserved on the banks of the north Tyne at Cilurnum.   It would seem that none of these smaller auxiliaries' forts boasted an amphitheatre for the amusement of the cohorts; but the legionary fortresses had them.   That at Chester has been located, though not, so far, excavated; but the amphitheatre at Caerleon has been completely exposed, and is by way of being a show-piece.

Inevitably sutlers' encampments, developing into civilian settlements, sprang up outside all but the very remotest Roman forts; such a settlement was called a *vicus*.   It had not only houses, but also temples, altars, and shops of various kinds selling foodstuffs, domestic utensils, tools, cutlery, boots and shoes and clothes generally, and even, apparently, souvenirs!   Here would live the wives and families of the soldiers in the fort, who would all have to live in barracks, though opportunities to visit their families would be frequent, as frequent as opportunities to drink and dice in the many inns to be found in a *vicus* (soldiers in the Roman army were great gamblers) or to buy provisions to supplement camp rations, and amuse themselves in off-duty hours in various ways according to their taste.   It would seem, however, that no *vicus* ever acquired a theatre; so that both soldiers and civilians evidently had to make their own amusement—not such a lost art in those days as it is in this era of bingo halls and television.

Some of these *vici* grew to considerable size.   Quite early in its history the one outside the fortress of the Sixth Legion at Eboracum became a *colonia*; but whether it, or indeed any of the towns of Roman Britain survived entire—that is to say preserving not only their buildings but some sort of corporate and organized life as self-governing urban communities through Anglo-Saxon into mediaeval and modern times—is 'not proven'. The fate of some towns—Verulamium, Viroconium, Calleva, Caistor-by-Norwich—is obvious: they became waste places where 'the wide walls fell; days of pestilence came; death swept away all the bravery of men; the grasp of the earth holds its mighty builders, who have perished and gone till now a hundred generations of men have died'.[1] The history of others, like London, York and Canterbury remains a mystery it seems we shall never now be able to solve.

[1] Anglo-Saxon poetry: *The Ruin.*

THE PLATES

1(*a*) MAIDEN CASTLE (pp. 5, 11)   The ramparts of the Iron Age hill-fort near Dorchester, showing the intricate system of defences at the western and eastern ends.   In times of peril the surrounding peasants would drive their sheep and cattle within the ramparts of the fort, and live there till the danger was past.   It was therefore more a corrall-cum-village than merely a fort.   The eastern entrance, which Vespasian's legionaries stormed, is on the right of the picture. A little to the NW of this may be seen the foundations of the Celtic temple and priest's house built in the mid-fourth century.

1(*b*) BASILICA WALL AND FORUM AT RATAE (LEICESTER) (p. 60)   Only part of the basilica wall has been excavated; the rest of the building is under the church. It would in Roman times have occupied the whole of this side of the forum; the other three sides would have contained shops and offices behind colonnaded walks, the side facing the basilica containing the entrance to the forum.

2(*a*) HEAD OF THE EMPEROR HADRIAN (p. 47)   This colossal second-century bronze head was found in the Thames at London Bridge.   The emperor's features as shown tally with other contemporary representations of him so that it may be considered a true likeness.   Classical in feeling and technique, it was no doubt made by a Greek artist in the imperial entourage.

2(*b*) HEAD OF CONSTANTINE THE GREAT (p. 134)   This early fourth-century head comes from Eboracum (York).   It is nearly life-size, carved in local stone.   It may have been erected in one of the public buildings of the legionary fortress, or in the colonia just outside it.   The sculptor was probably a Greek-trained Gaul in Constantine's household.

3(*a*) LULLINGSTONE CHRISTIAN FRESCO (p. 75)   Pieced together from the thousands of fragments of wall-plaster fallen from the upper room to the Deep Room below it at the Roman villa, this figure of a boy, one of six figures standing between painted columns in the *orant* attitude—the classical and early Christian attitude of prayer—has a curtain hanging behind him, possibly signifying that he has died, and belongs to the spirit world.   He wears a richly beaded, long robe of late classical fashion, and he may have been a member of the family who inhabited the house just before its destruction by fire.

3(*b*) MOSAIC FROM BRADING (p. 69)   This elaborate and highly individual mosaic floor lies in what was conceivably the State Room of the villa.   In the centre is a Medusa head, and radiating from this are four squares, one representing Ceres giving seed to Triptolemus, another a nymph dancing, watched by a shepherd, a third Hercules giving a double-headed axe to Omphale, Queen of Lydia, the fourth, largely destroyed, may have shown Daphne pursued by Apollo.   In the triangles are the Four Winds; and at either end are oblongs, one representing Tritons and mermaids merrymaking, the other the most unusual subject of the astrologer Hipparchus, bearded and semi-nude, seated and pointing with a wand to a globe supported on a tripod.   Above the globe is a pillar surmounted by a sundial, and to the astrologer's left is a vase with a pen(?) stuck in it.

4 THE HINTON ST. MARY MOSAIC (pp. 68, 70, 129)   This large, fourth-century mosaic (30 × 20 ft.), discovered in 1963, was designed as a continuous floor to fit two inter-communicating rooms.   The smaller room contained a roundel representing Bellerophon spearing the Chimaera; on either side are rectangles containing hunting scenes.   The larger room had four lunettes, one with a conventional tree, the other three hunting scenes; and in the centre roundel is a male head.   As this has behind it the Chi-Rho monogram, a Christian symbol, it almost certainly represents the head of Christ; if so, the four heads in the outer corners may represent the Evangelists.   This mosaic may contain, therefore, the earliest known representation of Christ in Britain, if not in the Roman Empire.

5(*a*) COIN OF CARAUSIUS (p. 104)   Carausius, the admiral put in charge of the fleet which had to deal with the menace of Saxon pirates towards the end of the third century, allowed himself to be proclaimed Emperor of Britain by the army, and ruled very efficiently from A.D. 286–293.

5(*b*) GOLD MEDALLION (p. 107) This medallion, found in Arras, was struck at Trier by Constantius Chlorus to commemorate the return of Britain to the Roman Empire after the usurpation of Carausius, and the defeat by Constantius of the admiral's successor, Allectus. Constantius is represented on horseback, greeted with outstretched arms by the city of London, personified as a woman, kneeling outside the city walls. A galley represents the river Thames. The inscription refers to the restoration of the light of Roman civilization.

6(*a*) HEAD OF MITHRAS (p. 123) Discovered in 1954 in the Walbrook Mithraeum, London. A late second-century work of Italian marble, of excellent quality and Mediterranean workmanship, obviously imported into Britain. Mithras, the cult image of the temple, was probably here represented in the act of slaying the sacred Bull, a symbolic act whereby Mithras brought life out of death, good out of evil, and light out of darkness. Only a Mediterranean artist, Greek or Greek-trained, could at this time have given the carving of the deity such emotional intensity as Mithras here possesses. The eyes were probably filled originally with enamel or glass paste.

6(*b*) HEAD OF SERAPIS (p. 133) Found with the head of Mithras in the cache of temple treasures in the Walbrook Mithraeum. Serapis was a Graeco-Egyptian god of fertility and the after-life, and the *modius*, or corn-measure, on his head is his accustomed attribute. This head is also of Italian marble, and expertly carved in the classical technique. There is nothing native about it.

7 MARBLE BUSTS FROM LULLINGSTONE (p. 134) These two busts, probably of early inhabitants of the villa, or their ancestors, were found by later residents abandoned in the house. They placed them in the Deep Room and set votive pots in front of them, no doubt as offerings to the *numina*—the departed spirits— which they represented. They are carved from Pentelic marble by Mediterranean sculptors, and represent Romans of some standing. They appear to be realistic likenesses, such as appealed to Romans of the second century A.D. Both seem to have been brought to Britain by the Romans who for a little while inhabited the villa and were not imported commercially.

8(*a*) MEDUSA HEAD (p. 137) This head, of Bath stone, now in the Roman Baths Museum, Bath, formed the central boss of a large circular shield in the pediment of the vanished classical temple of Sulis Minerva at Bath. The head of Medusa was frequently represented in Minerva's shield. The idea, therefore, is classical, and a male Medusa, with beard and moustache, is also not infrequent in the classical world. But unclassical is the flat, linear treatment of the subject, the interest shown in the interplay of light and shade to make a decorative pattern, the haunted and unearthly expression. These features are Celtic, and it is plain that the carver was a native Briton, or possibly a Gaul, trained in a classical school, but employing his own native Celtic idiom. It is an outstanding example of what could be achieved when classical standards and traditions were used by a native Celt of imagination and genius.

8(*b*) DISH FROM THE MILDENHALL TREASURE (p. 135) The group of 34 silver objects of table-ware, found in 1946, is of fourth-century date. The most outstanding object, perhaps executed in Gaul, is the large round dish with beaded rim and reliefs: the mask of Oceanus in the centre roundel, and two concentric zones of figure scenes picturing Nereids and sea-centaurs, Bacchus and his revel rout, Silenus, the drunken Hercules supported by satyrs, maenads and Pan.

9(*a*) HEAD OF A YOUTH (p. 138) Of British limestone this comes from Gloucester, and is another example of the happy aspects of the marriage of classical ideas and Celtic inventiveness and genius. It was evidently intended, in the classical manner, to be a realistic likeness of someone; the general outlines of the head and neck are classically realistic, but the slit mouth, the bulging eyeballs, the stylized ears and the ornamental pattern of the hair on the forehead are in the Celtic taste;

Celtic also is the aloof expression, the aura of dreaming spirituality which hovers over the head. It probably belongs to the first century A.D.

9(*b*) FUNERARY HEAD FROM TOWCESTER (p. 138)   This neckless head, of British stone, of the second or third century A.D. represents an underworld goddess.   The chin of the goddess rests directly on a base, often a feature of sepulchral monuments.   It makes several concessions to classical traditions, but the Celtic carver has given its staring eyes a barbaric intensity quite foreign to classical work, its woeful mouth and frowning brow bring a disturbing ferocity to what might have been a bland classical mask, and the whole face has a chilling, daemonic quality.

10(*a*) RECLINING RIVER GOD (p. 138)   This comes from Hadrian's Wall and belongs to the second or third century.   The pose and three-dimensional modelling of the deity are classical, but the substitution of the large mask of a water-deity for the more usual classical overturned urn upon which the god is leaning, and above all the pattern of lines of the drapery over the legs and the fine curving sweep of the cloak from the left shoulder are Celtic.   Another example of what could be produced by a native British artist of genius trained in the classical school but still imbued with Celtic feeling for ornament in its own right.

10(*b*) MINERVA   This damaged relief was found at Carrawburgh on Hadrian's Wall.   It is a Romano-British representation of the goddess with spear and shield and Gorgon's head breastplate.   The legs in the lower right hand corner probably belonged to Aesculapius, physician and god of healing, who perhaps stood beside her.   Though not a particularly skilful fusion of the classical and the Celtic, it has a certain native charm—frequently seen in lesser Romano-Celtic work.

11(*a*) HEAD OF A CELTIC DEITY (p. 139)   Found at Netherby, Cumberland, of the second or third century A.D., this is an example of a barbaric interpretation of a head, classical only in its three-dimensional character.   T. D. Kendrick remarks (*Anglo-Saxon Art*, p. 21): '[it] shows little but a totally un-Roman emotion expressed with a gaunt, savage symbolism. . . .   It is a relentless and implacable Celtic wonder, terrifying in its grimly supernatural power.   There is nothing here that is just decadent or unskilled classicism; on the contrary the work is conspicuously brilliant in its unimpaired native vigour, and, in fact, gains strength from a courageous and downright renunciation of the classical method.'

11(*b*) CASTOR-WARE BEAKER (p. 141)   From Colchester.   Castor ware was made from the late second century to the end of the Roman occupation.   It is named after the Northamptonshire potteries at which it was produced.   It has a dark, lustrous surface, and the pots are usually ornamented in barbotine with foliated scrolls or spirited animal figures.   This one shows a four-horse chariot-race, with the charioteer brandishing his whip and the horses straining towards the goal.

12 RELIEF FROM BREMENIUM (HIGH ROCHESTER) (p. 145)   A representation of three water-nymphs, or perhaps of Venus bathing, with her attendants.   The central figure is dressing her long hair, while a stream of water from an overturned urn flows behind her right leg; an attendant (?) on the right holds a jar in one hand and a tress of her hair in the other, on the left another female figure holds what may be a towel in front of her body.   An example of what happened when a native carver of little skill tried to imitate classical forms without the power or understanding to do more than produce caricatures lacking all classical dignity.

13(*a*) SEATED GODDESS   From Venta Silurum (Caerwent).   Native work in weathered sandstone of a goddess, perhaps a representation of a mother goddess.   Primitive, and owing nothing to classical traditions, it is reminiscent of figures carved in Roman Gaul before Romanization had swamped the native Celticism.

13(*b*) TOMBSTONE RELIEF (p. 142)   Commemorating a centurion of the 20th Legion and his wife.   The heads and stance of both figures have a certain Roman dignity; but the details of their garments and their over-short arms have only a geometrical value.   Kendrick (*Anglo-Saxon Art*, p. 23) refers to it as 'an essay in abstract art rather than a docile study in the classical manner', but many will consider it merely an inept copying of classical sepulchral portraitures.

1(a)

1(b)

2(a)

2(b)

3(b)

3(a)

5(a)

5(b)

6(a)

6(b)

8(a)

8(b)

9(a)

9(b)

10(a)

10(b)

11(a)

11(b)

13(b)

13(a)

X · THE ADVENTURE OF ALBINUS AND ITS CONSEQUENCES

We left the Brigantes tamed at last after their insurrection of 155; but the war against them, though successful, had unhappy results. We have seen how the governor, Lollius Urbicus, had been obliged because of the doings of the Brigantes to abandon his attempts to conquer the Lowlands while he devoted his energies to extinguishing the fires of revolt south of Hadrian's Wall. To put out those fires he must have drawn away from the Antonine Wall some part of the troops garrisoning it. Accordingly, the Antonine Wall being left as only an emasculated deterrent, revolts began again during the reign of Marcus Aurelius, with perpetual strife between Tyne and Solway.

Marcus Aurelius, the 'Philosopher Emperor', noted for his *Meditations* composed, as Gibbon says, 'in the tumult of a camp',[1] was not fortunate in his elder and only surviving son and successor, Commodus, who became emperor on the death of his father in 180. His bust indicates a weak, rather than an evil man, but he was self-indulgent as well as indecisive, and altogether unworthy to fill the position his father had left vacant. It is considered by Gibbon[2] among others, that with his succession degeneration of the Empire began, though of course there were other reasons for the decline, far more important. Trouble was beginning to stir everywhere, along all the six thousand miles of the frontier of the Roman Empire, from the Euphrates to Carlisle. Strong emperors, acutely conscious of their responsibilities, emperors of the calibre of Trajan, Hadrian, Antoninus Pius and Marcus Aurelius, a succession of outstanding Augusti, had illuminated the eighty-four years from 96 to 180, the greatest period of Roman imperial history; but with only one brief interval from 192 to 211 no such ruler arose till the third century had reached its penultimate decade.

[1] Gibbon, *Decline and Fall of the Roman Empire.*   [2] Ibid.

The first misfortune for Britain, almost as soon as the reign of Commodus had begun, was a disastrous raid of the tribes of Caledonia in which a Roman general was killed and his troops cut to pieces. This was the beginning of a war which lasted for six years and ended with the abandonment of the Antonine Wall. Its forts may have been stormed by the enemy, but it is more likely that they were evacuated in orderly fashion by their garrisons; from 187 the frontier was back again, where it was now destined to be till the end, at Hadrian's Wall. The Picts (the 'Painted Men', so called by the Britons, and by that name they are best known in history) then moved southward, and made permanent settlements in the lands between the two Walls. The war was punctuated by several mutinies in the army of Britain against their commanding officers; so that these years of trouble and unrest are not the happiest to record. During them, however, it appears that while these disturbances were agitating the north, the people of the south were leading ordered lives that took little heed of them.

But something was about to happen which, although no one could possibly have guessed it, was the shadow cast ahead upon the second century of a spectre that was to rise in the third, in the fourth and in the fifth, and which was to contribute in the fullness of time to the end of Roman rule in her most northerly province.

In the year 192 a certain Clodius Albinus was governor of Britain. He was well-born, and a wealthy man; but more important than this to the British legions, he was liberal handed and easy-tempered, and so was very popular with them, especially as he was a creditable soldier of some experience. He was not a very wise man, but he was an ambitious one; and when it happened that a rumour reached Britain that the emperor Commodus was dead Albinus's ambitions began to surge strongly within him. The army had made emperors before this; why should he not at least hint to the soldiers that if the imperial purple were offered him he would not be unwilling to consider the offer? Accordingly he did so.

The rumour, as it turned out, was false; but shortly after it had circulated the unpopular and unworthy Commodus did indeed die, assassinated by his courtiers. Then, with the 'golden age of the Antonines' at an end a confused year began having some resemblance to the 'year of the four emperors' which had followed the death of Nero. That year, however, had never descended to the disgraceful depths of this one. In Britain Albinus would have heard how in Rome the Praetorian Guards had actually put up the office of Divine Augustus and the Roman Empire to auction, to sell them to the highest bidder; and how the empire had been sold at a good price to an old incompetent called Didius Julianus (who, incidentally, never received the goods he had paid for). And as the army of Britain heard this astonishing news it immediately proclaimed its commander, Clodius Albinus, emperor.

How soon Albinus became aware that the other two great frontier armies of the Roman Empire—that in Syria, commanded by Pescennius Niger, and that on the Danube under the command of Lucius Septimius Severus, a native of the city of Leptis in the African province of Tripolitania— had done exactly the same thing is not known. What is known is that Severus was first in the field; and Albinus now heard that he and Pescennius Niger had both been forestalled. Obviously, whoever wanted to be emperor would have to fight for the honour. But while Albinus was making ready an offer reached him from Severus. That general agreed to recognize him as his 'Caesar'—which by this time had come to mean 'junior colleague', and was the recognized designation of the heir apparent. Commodus, for instance, at the age of five, had been called 'Caesar' by Marcus Aurelius. Severus also agreed to leave Albinus in complete control in Britain, in return for his alliance against Niger.

It has been said above that wisdom was not one of Albinus's characteristics. It seems not to have occurred to him that Severus was merely keeping him at bay for the time being, because he did not want a war on two fronts; he preferred not to fight two formidable armies, Albinus's and Niger's, at the same time, and that he feared the fierce British legions more than the oriental Syrian ones. His idea was to put the latter out of action before he was forced to the stiffer task of beating the former. Albinus evidently supposed that 'Caesar' was merely the prelude to 'Augustus', and that his turn would come eventually. He either forgot the existence of the two sons of Severus—Caracalla and Geta—or else, not unnaturally, these two being the sort of young men they were, thought them of no consequence. So, taken in by Severus's offer, he agreed to his terms, and quite enjoyed himself as Caesar in Britain, which he ruled with some success for just over three years—a period sometimes referred to as the 'First British Empire'.

By the time those three years had passed Severus had successfully concluded his operations against Niger, and had reorganized the eastern provinces. Albinus was now of no further use to him, and he turned his attention to eliminating him.

During the three years of his rule in Britain Albinus may or may not have been in treasonable communication with certain Roman senators anxious to be rid of Severus—his ambition may have urged him in that direction, but his enjoyment of the rôle of Caesar may just as easily have satisfied him: we do not know. But Severus wanted an excuse for getting this potential rival out of his way, and this was as good a one as any for attacking him. The next news that reached Albinus was that Severus had advanced with his army to the Alps, and had declared war on him.

Albinus at this was faced with two alternatives: to stay where he was and defend Britain, or to cross to Gaul in order to get, if he could, the supporting reinforcement of the legions there. It was the second alternative he chose. Knowing that his British legions would aid and abet him he declared himself Augustus—that is, emperor—and received their acclaim. Then taking all the troops that could be spared— or that he considered could be spared—for his adventure he crossed the Channel and called upon the Gauls to support his claim. Several Gallic troops rallied to him, and with his army thus reinforced he reached the Rhône and came to the city of Lugdunum (Lyons).

There a fierce and bloody battle was fought, in which for the first time since the accession of Vespasian—for a hundred and thirty years—rival Roman legions opposed each other in exhausting civil war. Severus's horse was killed under him, and he himself at one point was in mortal danger and escaped death only by flinging away his betraying imperial purple cloak. Albinus was no mean general, and the victory would have been his if reinforcements for Severus's broken troops had not arrived in the nick of time. Albinus was captured by the citizens of Lugdunum and executed—or as another account says he committed suicide. Such was the end of the 'First British Empire'. And this was the end also of a great number of soldiers who had formerly garrisoned Britain against her enemies and now lay dead beside the Rhône, never to return to British forts.

What, consequently, happened in the succeeding years in the north of Britain? Disaster. Albinus had drained away the life-blood of the northern garrisons in drawing off so many soldiers to Gaul to fight for his claim to rule the Roman Empire; one can imagine with what sentiments the enemies of Britain marked this. They had several old scores to pay off against the Romans. A fury of resentment had possessed them ever since the Wall had been built, and ever since Lollius Urbicus had seized their ancestors half a century ago and sent them to far off provinces in his attempts to subdue the lands between Tyne and Tweed in the 140's. Now was their chance to have their revenge. They broke through Hadrian's Wall, and at their leisure, apparently, wreaked their wrath upon this symbol of Roman conquest and power. Milecastles, turrets and forts from one end of the Wall to the other they wrecked with calculated fury. It is still possible to see at Housesteads (Vercovicium, the largest and strongest of all the forts on the Wall) that in days long past the enormous squared stones at the gateways have, course after course, been fiercely levered sideways out of their positions by human agency, not by Time. There is a milecastle a little to the west of Housesteads fort, and here we can see that the characteristic Roman piers of its north gate have been violently heaved away from the walls into which they were bonded, by stones snapped in two with the force with which they were moved. And although this cannot be seen now, the archaeologists who excavated the milecastle in modern times from the earth that the passage of fifteen centuries had piled upon it reported that the masonry above the floor had been so violently hurled down upon the flagstones paving it that the impact of their fall had tilted the flags up on edge.   Moreover in many places the actual Wall itself was overturned and destroyed to its foundations.

Destruction of this sort on such strong buildings needed time for its execution, and freedom from interference, and these were forthcoming.   There was no one of any conse-quence in the forts to oppose the destroyers; the garrisons had been withdrawn to fight elsewhere for a governor aiming to make himself emperor.   It was a story that was to be repeated in the years to come.

These destructive raids penetrated as far south as the legionary fortresses at York and Chester.   The walls of both were largely destroyed and had to be hastily rebuilt.   At Chester the builders, laying their hands on whatever suitable stone was nearest, took the very tombstones from the cemetery to rebuild the walls; and that is why we find such a splendid array of Roman memorials to the dead in the Grosvenor Museum in that city.   They were retrieved when the north wall of the former fortress was demolished towards the end of the nineteenth century.   The walled non-military towns—cantonal capitals and the like—do not seem to have been attacked at this time; partly because to take them would have meant siege-operations which the barbarians were not prepared for, and partly because the townsfolk would have been there to offer opposition.   In any case it was military installations that roused in the raiders the most furious resentment and lust for destruction.

After his defeat of Albinus, Severus, now undisputed emperor, in an effort to prevent any future governor becom-ing powerful enough to aim, as Albinus had done, at the imperial purple, had divided Britain into two parts: Upper and Lower Britain—*Superior* and *Inferior* in Latin, almost certainly meaning the higher, or mountainous land, and the plainland, since York was in Lower (Inferior) and Chester and Caerleon in Upper (Superior) Britain.   This arrange-ment was to make two co-ordinate and rival authorities in the province who would be a check on each other.   When the violent raids of the Picts began and they overran Hadrian's Wall and the lands south of it Virius Lupus was governor of Lower Britain; he bribed the raiders to make peace before putting in hand the rebuilding of the Wall. Such a peace was bound to last only a very short time.

His successor, Alfenius Senecio, successfully accomplished the rebuilding of the Wall but found the task of subduing the Picts beyond him, for we find him, in 208, reporting to Rome that the barbarians 'were in a state of turmoil and unrest, overrunning the country, driving off booty, and devastating every place; reinforcements were essential—or even'—here his urgency becomes apparent—'an expedition led by the emperor himself'.

Fortunately for Britain Severus happened to have no other war on hand at this time. In spite of the fact that he was an ageing man by now, still keen of intellect but suffering in health—he was liable to attacks of gout—he gathered together cohorts from the legions along the Rhine, and with Praetorians also accompanying him, speedily made his way across Gaul and landed in Britain. Also accompanying him were his two dissolute and unworthy sons, Caracalla and Geta, whom he was anxious to separate from evil influences in Rome. Neither had the slightest interest in the Caledonian War, or in Britain; but by their standards Geta must be considered the more fortunate of the two, for he was left to govern part of Britain while Caracalla had to accompany his father to the tribulations of the war in the north.

There are some who think that Severus's work in Britain was a failure because he never reoccupied the Lowlands or realized Agricola's dream of making Scotland part of the Empire. But before we agree with this view we should consider what it was he set out to do—what his real intentions were with regard to Scotland. If he had meant to annex the Lowlands, surely he would have reoccupied and re-garrisoned the Antonine Wall. But this he did not do, and did not attempt to do. It seems that his objective during his campaigns in Scotland—and he penetrated as far north as Aberdeenshire—was to punish the tribes who had risen consequent upon the departure of Albinus; to teach them that they could not with impunity defy the might of Rome; to lay waste the lands of those who had risen against that might, and depopulate the Lowlands so as to lessen the possibility of any future attacks upon Hadrian's Wall, which had never fallen before a frontal attack, and was captured by enemies only when its garrison was either withdrawn or in collusion with the enemies of Rome.   In short, to show the Picts and their confederates how dire were the consequences of rousing the wrath of Rome.

And in this he did succeed—at last, after long, wearying campaigns in which the enemy would never face him in battle, but persistently harassed him and his troops wherever they were, laying ambushes for them, and making as wearisome and laborious as their skill in guerrilla tactics enabled them to do, their marches, their efforts to build bridges over rivers and passages across swamps and marshes and their cutting away of obstructing trees and thickets.   Had Severus been a commander of less tough fibre and grim determination he must have given up long before the year 210.   As it was, he had, by that year, as he had meant to do, inflicted such revenge upon the barbarians for their former outrages and so broken their spirit that they sued for peace.

Negotiations for a settlement began; but the emperor, already a sick man when he first arrived in Britain, was now a broken one.   Worn out by his arduous marches against an enemy 'who never stood still to be hit'[1] and the rigours of both climate and terrain, and bitterly disappointed in his elder son, Caracalla, who not only displayed no aptitude for war, but tried to sow disaffection amongst the soldiers and to tamper with their loyalty to his father, he was not in a fit state to endure the final blow which came with a report that the barbarians had again attacked the garrisons he had left in the forts on the road between the Lowlands and Corbridge.   He died in York in 211.   Immediately his successor, Caracalla, patched up a peace with the barbarians, withdrew his father's garrisons from the Lowland forts, and speedily departed for Rome.   The line of Roman defence in Britain was back once more at Hadrian's Wall.

That frontier-line held firm.   It is clear, from the thoroughness with which Severus, prior to his arrival in Britain, had ordered the Wall to be restored that he had all

---

[1] Collingwood.

along intended it to be the frontier-line of the province.
Indeed, so substantial and fundamental had been his restoration of the Wall that in some ancient and many of the older
modern histories of Roman Britain we find it stated that
Severus was its original builder in the first decade of the
third century. This is not true, and modern scholarship
and archaeology have proved that the first builder was the
emperor after whom we now name the Wall—Hadrian, and
no other. But when we consider the extent and magnitude
of the reconstruction that was necessary after the onslaught
upon it of the northern tribes we can see how easy it was for
this mistaken attribution to Severus to arise. Indeed in
many places Lupus and Senecio actually did have to rebuild
the Wall from its very foundations. No deviation was
made anywhere from the line Hadrian had originally
mapped out, and his foundations were strictly adhered to.
But the ruins we see along Hadrian's Wall today belong
largely to the years 198 to 208, not to 121 to 128.

The work was so well done that after the death of Severus
and the departure of Caracalla Britain enjoyed more than a
century of peace from the Caledonians. There may have
been a few raids from the north, but if there were they must
have been of secondary importance, for history says nothing
of them.

It was a different story in the rest of the Roman domains.
When one reads the history of the third century one wonders
how it was that the Roman Empire survived at all. The
mounting storm that began to gather after Severus's death
broke in devastating fury soon after 240, when barbarians
began pouring in a simultaneous flood over nearly every
frontier. In the west they swarmed over the Rhine, murdering and pillaging as they went, and made their swift and
ruinous way through Switzerland and Gaul. At the same
time the Franks—a confederation of German tribes—taking
to the sea, began to raid the east coast of the Roman province
of Spain. In the north-east of Europe the Goths came down
the valleys of the Dneiper, the Dneister and the Danube to
the Black Sea, defeating Roman armies on the way and
killing the Emperor Decius. They sacked peaceful towns in
Asia Minor, and appearing on the Aegean Sea overran the

Greek islands.   In the east the Sassanids, a dynasty which had eliminated Parthia and founded the new Persian king-dom, and which was now represented by King Sapor I, not only defeated Roman armies confronting them but took the Roman emperor Valerian prisoner, and kept him a captive till his death.   And the Emperor Aurelian was forced to withdraw behind the Danube and surrender the province of Dacia to the barbarians—destined to be never again recovered.

Nor was this all.   Every succeeding emperor—and they succeeded each other with great rapidity, most of them being murdered by their successors—had to deal with revolting generals within their own ranks, aspirants to the imperial throne.   When they should have been facing the enemy beyond the frontiers the emperors were having to deal with the enemies in their very midst.   Nor could the legions, as they had done of old, be rapidly moved from their stations to reinforce danger spots: the danger spots were everywhere, the legions were wanted east and west and north and south at once.   And those legions, too, becoming already in the third century filled with barbarian elements which were to increase as time went on, had not that spirit of loyalty to the emperor and devotion to all Rome stood for which they had had in days gone by.   What should barbaric soldiers from far distant federated tribes know or care about the majesty and divinity of the City by the Tiber, founded a thousand years ago by the will of the gods themselves? Their loyalty was to their commander; all their devotion was centred on him, the tangible, visible man, not on an intangible, invisible and to them inexplicable spirit of Rome.

During the dark years 250 to 270 pretenders and claimants to Empire sprang up everywhere.   Sometimes they were local leaders who tried to keep invaders at bay on what might be called the outer perimeter of the Empire, and who organized their own defence because they knew that the legitimate emperor struggling at the Empire's centre was unable to help them; they had no intention of seceding from the beleaguered Empire, and throwing in their lot with the barbarians.   This happened in Gaul, where Postumus and Tetricus were elevated by discontented army groups and considered themselves emperors of what is known as 'the empire of Gaul'. Britain was a willing participant in this secessionist 'empire', and acquiesced readily in the elevation of Postumus and his successor; became, in fact, part of the empire of Gaul. Eventually, in 274, after the empire of Gaul had lasted sixteen years, Tetricus submitted to the legitimate emperor, Aurelian. Britain then took a more prominent part in revolt, led by Bonosus and Proculus. Bonosus, though his mother was a Gaul, had a British father, and is therefore considered a Briton; he is the first British pretender to the imperial purple. He and Proculus proclaimed themselves emperors at Cologne, and in the violent confusion of the times even managed to keep that title for a while. But when the legitimate emperor, Probus (276–82), marched against them they were both defeated and killed. Another pretender, who remains strangely anonymous, was immediately set up by the Britons, but he was treacherously murdered, and after his death the province of Britain returned to its allegiance. All along it seems that the defection of Britain and Gaul was not a rebellion of natives against the Roman imperial system; only a clinging to usurpers, unrecognized by Rome, who seemed likely to give them protection against enemy attacks. In any case Britain appears to have re-entered the imperial fold contentedly enough.

Britain seems to have suffered less than almost any other Roman province from the catastrophic upheavals of this calamitous third century. Protected by Hadrian's Wall, as rebuilt and regarrisoned by Severus, the province seems to have been enviably unique in remaining virtually unmolested by any serious landward attacks throughout the middle decades of the third century. These years appear to have been, as far as the civilian population was concerned, an even prosperous time, at any rate in the countryside. Only in the towns have signs been discovered of any effects upon Britain of the deplorable economic situation in the Empire at large which accompanied the wasting of lands and cities in war, the disruption of trade and communications and the devaluation of the currency. The decay of Britain's towns is proved to us today by the excavations of archaeologists.

At Verulamium in the mid-third century the area in front of the stage of the theatre was buried, as excavation has shown, many feet deep in tipped rubbish—a fine public building had become a refuse dump.   At Viroconium the forum was accidentally burnt down towards the end of the century, and although it was the centre of the civic life of the town it was never rebuilt.   The road alongside the forum and close to the basilica at Ratae (Leicester) was allowed to fall into squalid disrepair.   And so the tale goes on.   Perhaps the councillors, the decurions, responsible for the maintenance of municipal services, streets and pathways and public buildings, impoverished by the decline in trade owing to the troubles abroad, or by the heavy taxation which war always brings in its train, shirked their civic duties and at the earliest opportunity retired to their country estates where life was easier and the demand upon their finances less severe; or perhaps there were other reasons for this decay of the towns.   But as it occurs in this ruinous third century it would be the effect upon Britain of the ills of the Roman Empire everywhere else.

XI · THE BEGINNING OF A NEW DANGER

The tide began to turn at last with the advent to power of the four successive 'soldier-emperors'—Claudius II, Aurelian, Tacitus and Probus. They were effective between them in forcing back the invaders, re-occupying most of the territory which had been overrun by them, and propping up the tottering walls of Roman imperial power just as they had seemed about to crash down in irreparable ruin. The situation was finally retrieved towards the end of the century, and a reorganization was effected which played an important part in prolonging the life of the western half of the Empire for nearly two centuries, and the eastern for over a thousand years. It was an Illyrian farmer's son who by sheer military ability had risen to be governor of Moesia, a province in what is now the Balkans, and who was acclaimed emperor by the army in 284, who achieved this. His name was Diocletian.

He, judging that the vast extent of the Roman Empire represented a burden that was too heavy for one ruler to bear unaided, and judging also that it was time a remedy was found for such disputes over the succession as had caused discord and war throughout the third century, disturbing the peace of much of the Roman world and weakening its efficiency, devised a system (the 'Tetrarchy') whereby the administration of the Empire should be divided between four partners—two senior, with the title of Augustus, and two junior, with subordinate authority, styled Caesars. One Augustus was to rule the eastern half of the Empire (all the lands east of the Adriatic Sea) with his capital at Nicomedia, the other the western half, his capital being Mediolanum (Milan), not Rome any longer, though Rome always retained its ancient prestige. One Caesar, meanwhile, was to be in charge of what we now call the Balkan Peninsula, with his capital at Sirmium (Mitrovitza); the other admini-stered Gaul (which included Britain) and Spain with

Treveri (Trier) on the Moselle as his capital. Diocletian himself, ruling from Nicomedia, was supreme Augustus. The other Augustus, Maximian, was referred to as his 'colleague'. Galerius was Caesar of the Balkan provinces; and—the one who mostly concerns us in continuing the story of Britain—Constantius Chlorus (the 'Sallow-complexioned') was Caesar in the west, ruling Spain, Gaul and Britain.

Diocletian had seen the danger of placing too much power, especially military power, in the hands of provincial governors. The governors had been commanders-in-chief of the army of the province they administered, and if the army was behind them they had been able, as we have seen in the case of Albinus—and it had happened time and time again throughout the third century—to reach out for the imperial purple with considerable hope of success. Diocletian therefore took special care to separate military from civil power. No unit of territory was to be left so large that it would make a governor of it as dangerously powerful as they had been hitherto, and therefore the provinces were splintered, as it were, into minor units still called provinces, while the sum total of them all, the former province, was to be known as a 'diocese'. Britain was divided into four (much later a fifth was added) provinces[1] and was henceforth referred to as a diocese of the praefecture of Gaul. Like all the other dioceses of the Empire it was regulated no longer by a governor, but by a *vicarius*, a civilian official responsible for all the administrative and financial machinery of government, but having no control over the officers who commanded the army of Britain. Under the *vicarius* were four subordinate civilian governors, one for each of the four new and smaller provinces—all potential rivals, likely to keep a check on each other.

It was about this time that a new danger began to loom upon the British horizon—the first appearance of Teutonic marauders—Saxon and Frankish pirates—off the British and Gallic coasts. It is not known why these German

---

[1] The names of the four provinces were: Britannia Prima, Britannia Secunda, Maxima Caesariensis, Flavia Caesariensis. We do not know the areas these covered. The later added fifth province was an unidentifiable tract of land called Valentia.

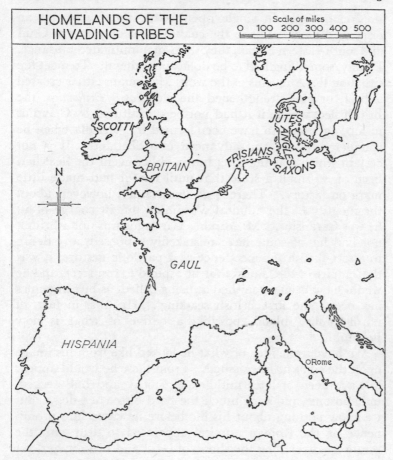

HOMELANDS OF THE
INVADING TRIBES

Scale of miles
0   100   200   300   400   500

barbarians had not begun their depradations earlier, or why
they began them at all; but the whole of the Germanic
world had been in a state of more or less active unrest for
centuries, and perhaps the wild hordes lurking in their
impenetrable forests on the frontiers of the Empire had
marked the third-century degeneration and thought that
now was their chance, if ever, to loot and plunder the rich
lands of the civilized.

These Teutonic hordes attacking Gaul and Britain were,
at this period, in no sense invaders.   They came to raid and
carry off booty, with no ideas at present of settlement, and

they came only in single open boats; they were not an
organized navy.   But to the coastal areas of northern Gaul
and south-eastern Britain they were an unmitigated nuisance.
Plainly, something had to be done about them.   To meet the
situation the Augustus of the west, Maximian, either created
a fleet, or else strengthened the old *Classis Britannica*, the
British fleet which, if it had not been instituted by Claudius
in A.D. 43, seems to have been formed by Agricola when he
conquered Wales and advanced into Scotland.   It is not
certain which was the case; but in either event the fleet had
been on so small a scale that until now it had made little
mark on history.   There is no uncertainty, however, about
the identity of the admiral Maximian put in charge of it:
he was Carausius.   M. Aurelius Carausius was not a Briton,
nor had he, as some have mistakenly supposed, any desire
to assert British independence as a patriotic gesture; it was
the 'empire of the Gauls' that he aspired to resurrect, and he
would have been astonished at being called, as he sometimes
has been, 'the first British sea-king'.   He was, in fact, of
north-Gaulish blood, possibly a native of what is now
Belgium.

We have some idea of what he looked like from his image
upon the coins he later issued.   From these he would appear
to have been of later middle-age, stocky and bull-necked,
unhandsome and very much the hard-bitten sea-dog.   But
we know nothing about his life before he came into promi-
nence as the Roman admiral appointed to deal with the
pirate menace along the shores of Gaul and Britain; and yet
he must have been an exceptional man.   He was certainly
an exceptional seaman and naval tactician, of whom there
are not many in the annals of Rome.

The early days of his command were crowned with great
success.   Making his headquarters at Gessoriacum (Bou-
logne) where was the arsenal of his fleet, he attacked the
boats of many of the pirates and destroyed them; he
recovered a good deal of the plunder they were carrying off.
But presently it began to be rumoured that his naval skill
was not matched by his integrity.   A report reached
Maximian that Carausius did not seem very eager to prevent
the pirates from raiding the British and Gallic shores; he

preferred, it was said, to let them raid, and then attack them when they were laden with loot, so that he might seize it. That would not have mattered so much if he had either returned the loot to those who had been robbed of it, or failing that, had handed it over to the imperial treasury. But he did neither of these things. He kept it for himself and his crews. Indeed, the accusations went even further, and maintained that he had a secret understanding with some of the pirates. Hearing all this Maximian forthwith made ready to arrest him and bring him to trial, and execution.

Faced with this situation Carausius—boldness seems to have been one of his outstanding characteristics, along with unscrupulousness—gathered his adherents around him, crossed from Gaul to Britain, and proclaimed himself emperor of the diocese, as Albinus had done a century before, appealing to the three legions there to support him. Before long the whole island had joined him.

His aim, as we have said, was not to be merely emperor of Britain, but emperor of all Gaul; and from Gessoriacum he tried to extend his power beyond a strip of the northern coastline. He tried also to win over to his side the legions garrisoning the Rhine, but was unable to move their loyalty. As soon as Maximian had a fleet ready to deal with the usurper he attacked him at sea, but was defeated—his unskilful, untrained sailors were no match for the seamanship of Carausius and his crews, especially in the sort of bad weather which it was Maximian's misfortune to encounter during this naval battle. Faced with Carausius's unshaken command of the sea Maximian and the supreme Augustus, Diocletian, harassed as they were by other foes at this time, thought it expedient to make peace with Carausius until a more propitious moment for dealing with him arrived. Against their will, but forced by necessity, they confirmed him in his possession of Britain, placed under his command the south shore of the English Channel (the *Fretum Gallicum*) and acknowledged him as their colleague, provided he ceased pursuing further his ambitions in Gaul. This is how it comes about that there exist coins of the year 289 struck with the busts of the three emperors side by side.

H

Carausius ruled *de jure* as an emperor in Britain for seven years, from 286 to 293, as successful in civil government as he was in naval warfare. During those seven years he increased his fleet, and taking no chances, got as large an army as possible behind him, raising new levies and hiring a large force of Frankish mercenaries, as if he realized the real insecurity of his position and the lack of sincerity of the two Augusti. The seven years were marked by peace and prosperity. Carausius ruled Britain well, and his fleet and command of the seas kept the realm, during that period, safe from the Saxons. In fact there are some indications that he obtained a great victory over them; and there are those who ascribe to him the building of that great defensive line, the Saxon Shore forts. But as it is more probable that Constantius Chlorus was responsible for their erection, we will defer further mention of them for a while. Yet whether Carausius did or did not conceive the idea of these forts, certain it is that after this time we hear no more of Saxon raids on Britain for over half a century. As for the Franks, Carausius had not only made peace with them but had kept many of them as auxiliaries. And from the fact that there are no reports of attacks upon Hadrian's Wall during those seven years of Carausius's rule we may assume that the admiral's efficiency extended to the firm garrisoning of the Wall forts also.

But in 292 the wars which had kept Diocletian and Maximian busy elsewhere were ended, and they had time at last to deal with one they had never ceased privately to consider a usurper. They declared war on Carausius; and Maximian's junior colleague, his 'Caesar', Constantius Chlorus in command of Transalpine Gaul, began to advance against him. Carausius's command of the sea again baulked those opposing him. Even at the end of two years Constantius Chlorus had been able to achieve nothing against the 'emperor of Britain' except the capture, after a long siege, of his naval base at Gessoriacum. The able admiral was more than a match for the Caesar; and it looked as if the stalemate might last years.

The end came very suddenly. Carausius was murdered by his treasury official, Allectus—to escape punishment for his own irregular acts, it was said—and his place and power were immediately seized by the murderer.

Allectus was a man of very different stamp from Carausius and far inferior to him in every way. He had, however, made his preparations. He had won over part of the army Carausius had raised, and managed to reign for three years—the time required by Constantius Chlorus for building fleets in all the harbours of northern Gaul. In 296 Constantius sailed for Britain. Abandoning his fleet when he learnt that a division of Constantius's under the prefect Asclepiodotus had slipped past him in a fog off the Isle of Wight, Allectus, with a force made up largely of Frankish mercenaries because he was unable to trust the legions, met Constantius somewhere west of London—maybe in Wiltshire—and in the ensuing battle he was decisively beaten and killed—unnoticed, it is said—in the rout which followed.

None of the Britons seem to have mourned his demise. When Constantius Chlorus advanced on London he was received with open arms by the citizens. So far from bewailing the loss of their three-year 'emperor', they hailed the Caesar as *Redditor Lucis Aeternae*—Restorer of the Eternal Light—that is, of Roman civilization, as those glad to have done with independence, and to be back again in the imperial fold. There exists a gold medallion of this year—296—found in modern times at Arras, which represents Constantius, spear in hand, riding on horseback beside the river Thames on which is an oared galley, towards the turreted gate of London; before the gate kneels a female figure, plainly representing the Genius of London, welcoming him with outstretched hands.

In gathering together all the troops he could muster to make his stand against the invading Caesar Allectus had done as Albinus had done before him, a hundred years previously: he had seriously depleted the garrisons along Hadrian's Wall. The result in 296, though not quite as catastrophic, was similar to that in 197. The northern barbarians broke through Hadrian's Wall again, and wrought havoc there. As Severus had done long before so Constantius did again now, rebuilt the shattered ruins, and made the frontier secure once more. He also rebuilt the fortress of Eboracum, and the so-called 'Multangular' tower which we can still see in the grounds of the York Philosophical Society was erected by him, although now the upper part of it is mediaeval.

History seemed to be repeating itself; for in 306, after the Wall had been for the second time restored, Constantius Chlorus returned to Britain to undertake a punitive war, as Severus had done, against the Lowland tribes. This time we are definitely told that his intentions were punitive, and that he had no thought of annexing territory; his aim was certainly what we can only assume Severus's was. His son Constantine was present when he won a great victory which concluded his campaigns; and then, still strangely following in Severus's footsteps, ninety-five years after Severus he also died in York—in 306.

Since Constantius did so much to make all the frontiers of Britain secure—including the west coasts, for new enemies were beginning to arise on that side of the island in the shape of raiders from Ireland, called, rather confusingly to us, *Scotti*—it seems reasonable to suppose that it was Constantius rather than Carausius who fortified the coast of south-east Britain, from the Wash to the Solent, with the 'Forts of the Saxon Shore'. Four of these exist in substantial ruin to this day at Burgh Castle in Suffolk, Richborough in Kent, Pevensey in Sussex and Portchester in Hampshire; the others at Brancaster, Walton Castle, Bradwell-on-Sea, Reculver, Dover and Lympne have either been wholly or in large part swallowed up by the encroaching sea, torn down to furnish material for later buildings, tumbled about by landslides, or have left only slight, almost indistinguishable traces.

These forts were designed to be the answer to the troubles of the age in Britain—the menace of Saxon and Frankish raids. To Constantius it evidently seemed undesirable or dangerous ever again to entrust to one man the command of such an efficient and powerful weapon as the *Classis Britannica* had been, so as to fight the barbarians at sea and prevent them from landing at all. He broke it up by distributing its personnel among smaller naval squadrons whose business it was merely to patrol the coasts and report to base any threatening movements of the enemy. Their bases were the forts of the Saxon Shore, built close to the coast on harbours or natural inlets of the sea. The south-east coastline has altered since Roman times, and while in some places—Walton and Reculver, for instance—the sea has encroached and entirely or partly obliterated the fort, in others, as at Pevensey and Lympne, it has receded and left the forts high and dry over a mile from the shore.

The garrisons of the forts were military; we even hear of the Second Legion being transferred, late in the Roman period, from the borders of Wales to Richborough in Kent, though we do not know exactly the date of its move. Usually, however, the garrisons were composed of auxiliaries.

The forts of the Saxon Shore were different from the earlier forts inland, and along Hadrian's Wall. They were much larger, for one thing; and their defensive walls were more massive, ten to fourteen feet thick, and reinforced with bastions in most cases to take the heavy artillery of the age and to enfilade the walls whenever the enemy effected a landing and presumed to attack them. At Richborough, Pevensey, Burgh Castle and Portchester these walls still stand in part to an impressive height of sixteen to twenty feet. They were found still so serviceable eight hundred years after their erection that the Norman invaders repaired and used them as enceinte walls for the castles they built in a corner of them at Pevensey and Portchester—these castles still stand. Nothing brings home to us a more vivid realization of the actuality of the presence of the Romans in our land fifteen hundred years ago than the sight of these stout walls rising above the waters of the Waveney, the marshes of Thanet or Pevensey, or on the skirts of Portsmouth Harbour.

Yet they represent a mistaken strategy. If the Saxons were to be conquered at all, they should have been met out at sea and conquered before they had had a chance to land— with hindsight we can see that now. The mistake might not have been so important in earlier days, when there were men enough to man in force all the long frontiers of the Roman Empire; but at the beginning of the fourth century there were not men enough. The frontier in south-east Britain held for a while only because the Saxons were for the

next half-century quiescent, or quiescent enough to be
deterred by this grim-looking line of fortifications, or still
thinking only of booty, not settlement in the land. The
fact remains that we hear no more of them for sixty years
after the death of Constantius.

A new officer was created to command this range of
coastal defences. He was called *Comes Litoris Saxonici*—
Count of the Saxon Shore. His counterpart in the north,
who from his base at the fortress of Eboracum now commanded all the northern defences, including Hadrian's
Wall, was called *Dux Britanniarum*—Duke of the Britains,
that is, the four provinces into which the diocese had now
been divided.[1]

Diocletian's aim to separate the military command from
the civilian, and where possible to weaken the former, so
that no one man should be powerful enough to cause the
civil wars which had tortured the years of the third century,
was thus confirmed in Britain, where even the naval command was separated from the military, and the commander
of the legions was no longer the same man as the governor.

Possibly it was not Constantius, but his son Constantine
who created these commands. Diocletian died in 305, a
year before Constantius; and not long after his death the
Tetrarchy collapsed under the overwhelming personality and
ambitions of Constantine. In 305 both the Augusti had
abdicated, and their Caesars had become Augusti in their
stead, according to the rule, making Constantius Chlorus
emperor of the West; when Constantius Chlorus died the
following year the troops in Britain declared Constantine
Augustus in his father's place, without consulting anybody,
least of all the elder Augustus, now Galerius. Naturally
Constantine had to fight for his position, and after eliminating his rivals he became sole ruler of the Roman world in
324.

He reigned till 337, and developed in Britain and elsewhere
many of Diocletian's reforms, but the Tetrarchy was henceforth a dead letter; Constantine abandoned the system of
Augusti and Caesars, and aimed at a dynastic succession,

---

[1] The Diocletian divisions of Britain were introduced after the death of
Allectus.

with the Empire divided at his death among his three
sons. But while he yet lived he was responsible for
two events of lasting importance. He shifted the capital
of the Empire from the West to the city which he founded
in the East, on the site of the ancient Greek colony of
Byzantium, on the Golden Horn near the entrance to the
Black Sea, and called it 'the city of Constantine'—Constantinople. And he came to terms with Christianity. His
motives in doing so were more likely to have been political
than devotional, for the times demanded that all discord
within the Empire should cease, and that the Roman world
should present a united front against its steadily encroaching
enemies; but it is only fair to state that not everyone agrees
with this view. In any case, his motives did not affect the
outcome. From now on, with only one short partial inter-
ruption of no lasting consequence during the years 361 to
363, when Julian the Apostate was emperor, Christianity
was supported by the State, and at last became the official
religion of the Empire, though the existence of paganism was
tolerated side by side with it.

For Britain the years from Constantine's accession to just
past the middle of the fourth century were an era of peace
and prosperity—a 'Golden Age', if that term may be
applied to any age known to history. During those fifty
years villa-life in the country flourished, and those who
enjoyed it must have supposed, in the absence of any disturbance to break the even tenor of their days, that the millen-
nium had come, and that this state would last forever. And
having reached these halcyon days, this golden late summer
before the autumn storms presaging the darkness and death
of winter, we may again pause to consider two things of
importance in the lives of the people of Britain: Religion and
Art.

XII · RELIGION IN ROMAN BRITAIN

When the Romans conquered Britain all they required of the natives in the sphere of religion was participation in the cult of the emperor—a cult which was intended to serve as a unifying focus of loyalty—and the rejection of any worship, such as Druidism, which was distinguished by an intolerant nationalism antagonistic to imperial policy. When Druidism had been destroyed Rome offered no further opposition to any of the vast array of native gods which aroused the enthusiasm or gained the favour and worship of those inhabiting the land. It is sometimes forgotten that in matters of religion the Romans were, perhaps, the most easy-going and tolerant of any power that has ever guided an empire. Only when a religion seemed to them antagonistic to the safety and welfare of the State, especially as symbolized by its chief representative, the emperor, did they forbid, or endeavour to forbid, the practice of it. It was for this reason that they persecuted Christianity; and even then the persecution was sporadic, much influenced by the temper prevailing at certain times, and always due ultimately to the fact that while the Christians were thinking in spiritual, the Romans were thinking in political terms, and neither came anywhere near comprehending the standpoint of the other.

On their side the Britons had no objection to participating in the cult of the emperor. It entailed only a formal act which lay lightly upon the surface of their personal views and religious practices. Nor did they take any more exception to the Roman gods than the Romans took to the Celtic ones. In fact, one tended to merge into the other, and the history of Romano-British religion becomes largely a blend of two cultures in which, in the end, the Celtic element almost submerges the Roman.

There were, in the first decades after the conquest, certain individuals (like Cogidubnus of the Regnenses) who were

either anxious to gain the favour of the conquerors or else
carried away on the impetus of a fashion for anything
Roman. These, as one aspect of their apeing of the
Romans, worshipped pure Roman gods—Jupiter, Juno,
Minerva, Apollo and the rest of them; but this was not
general. Among civilians at least the tendency soon died
away, and Celtic forms of worship, quite unromanized,
were followed everywhere outside the military areas. In
those, in the forts and fortresses of the north, we know from
inscriptions and inscribed altars that the official gods of
Rome—as might be expected—were worshipped especially
by the officers of the army, who in earlier times would have
been exclusively Italian-born Romans. But it is significant
that most of these inscriptions belong to the second century.
As the years passed by they become rarer, and by the middle
of the fourth century they have all but vanished. This is in
keeping with the increasing barbarization of the Roman
armies in the later Empire, when even high commands were
given—as in the case we shall mention presently of Stilicho,
a Vandal—to non-Romans.

But this worship of the official gods of Rome had long since
become dry and empty, a sterile formality even to the
Romans themselves. The dedication of altars to them by the
army were merely official public acts in which the soldiery,
Roman and native, joined as a matter of course, as they
automatically answered to the bugle-call, but which did not
affect their emotions or touch their hearts. Most of the
official military altars were dedicated to the supreme Roman
god and guardian deity of the Roman state, Iuppiter Optimus Maximus, and we know of one official ceremony in this
connection which took place on the Kalends of January
(the first of January) each year. On the parade ground, in
the sight of all the troops, the officer commanding would set
up an altar to Iuppiter Optimus Maximus, and when it had
been dedicated he would with reverent solemnity bury the
altar of the year before underground. There must be quite
a cache of buried Roman altars near former military stations
if only we knew exactly where to dig for them.

There was nothing Celtic about this formal, official worship of Jupiter; and though Mercury was worshipped for

good luck both by the rank and file of the army and by civilians—chiefly traders—and Hercules, hero and demi-god, Neptune, lord of all waters, and Silvanus, god of the wild and of hunting, had at any rate nominal British devotees, none of these seems ever to have been absorbed into the native religion.   Mars, however, does appear to have become more of a living reality to the common soldier—but only after he had been equated with various native gods—Belatucadrus, Camulus, Cocidius and Corotiacus (latinized versions of Celtic names which the Romans found it impossible both to pronounce and to decline).

But not even in the army were the native gods of Celtic, Germanic or any other origin persecuted.   On the parade ground the soldier paid formal reverence to Jupiter, to the *numen* (guardian angel, as a Christian would have said) of the emperor, to the protective deities of the state and to the regimental standards; once outside the fort all his reverence was given to the gods of his homeland.   We remember that the auxiliary cohorts and *alae* especially were a cosmopolitan crowd, formed of inhabitants of all the provinces of the Roman Empire; when they were brought to Britain they brought their gods with them.   The Tungrians brought Viradechthis and Harimella, the Vangiones of the Middle Rhine brought Mogons, the Gauls of the Lower Rhine brought their Matres Alateivae, the Frisians from across the Rhine brought Mars Thincsus with his attendant female goddesses or sprites, the Alaisiagae, the Syrian archers brought their Dea Hammia.   The only Roman things about the worship of these deities with the uncouth names were their inscribed dedications, which were always in Latin (sometimes misspelt and ungrammatical) and the fact that any images that were made of them appeared in what was at least intended to be classical form.

But the general mass of the people in town and country, artisans and shopkeepers, dwellers in the farmhouse villas large and small and the peasants who cultivated the soil and lived in the round, thatched huts or barn-like appendages to the villas, worshipped the Celtic gods of their fathers, and though the most romanized of them in the towns of the south-east paid lip-service, like the army, to the

Roman gods and the *numen Augusti*, to whom the welfare and salvation of the State were due, their real allegiance was to the old Celtic gods. Gods—in the plural, be it remarked. The noteworthy thing about the native religion is that no god was dominant in the Celtic pantheon, no one god seems to have been worshipped everywhere in the island. The worship of the gods was not organized, as it had been in Rome. Cults of particular gods were for the most part local. Sometimes the locality was wide. Thus we have Brigantia, a personification of the tutelary spirit of the Brigantes, who is represented in one statue we have of her as a territorial goddess wearing a mural crown, a war-goddess dressed like a Roman Minerva (but with an auxiliary, not a legionary helmet) and a Victory with wings, all rolled into one; she seems, judging from dedications to her, to have been worshipped from the southern Pennines to Hadrian's Wall. On the other hand we have the extremely localized deity of the sacred spring, Coventina, worshipped apparently only at Carrawburgh, on the Wall; she is represented reclining, sometimes in triplicate to emphasize her power, on a leaf. She evidently brought good fortune to her devotees. The soldiers in the adjacent fort of Brocolitia used to throw coins 'for luck' into the well in the centre of her shrine, and when the sacred basin was excavated in modern times there were found in it over thirteen thousand coins, mostly silver and bronze though four were of gold, together with a mass of votive objects—precious stones, brooches, jars and incense-burners. In Northumbria Matunus, 'the kindly one', was worshipped; Anocitius and Antenociticus had their temple at Benwell, also on the Wall.

These are all deities localized in the north. We do not know so much about the local gods of the south. The explanation is not far to seek. The inscribed stone altars, by which alone we know them, have in the north, a region rich in stone, been more often left where they were; in the more stoneless south altars that once must have existed have disappeared because the stone of which they were made was seized and turned to building use long ago, in the ages when men had forgotten or never known the Roman art of brick-making.

Nevertheless, we have knowledge of some local Celtic gods of the south.   There must be few people who have not heard of Sul, or Sulis, goddess of the hot springs at Bath, and perhaps also tutelary deity of the river Avon.   The Romans discovered the curative properties of those hot springs; they built a temple in the classical style near them, and the town —a small one—of Aquae Sulis, and they resorted to it in large numbers in search of health and relaxation and amusement.   Bath's first fashionable era lies in Roman times; and as so many Romans frequented the town Sulis was soon equated with Minerva.   But though the town was called 'Waters of Sulis' it was never called 'Waters of Minerva'; the temple erected close by the thermae was called the temple of Sulis Minerva, never of Minerva alone. The Celtic goddess allowed some parity of esteem, but did not brook expulsion.   This is the case with all the Celtic deities.   They were never ousted from their seats, though they might occasionally consent to share them with the Roman outsider.

The temple of Sul (or Sulis) Minerva at Bath may have been built by the Romans over a native Celtic shrine already sacred to water deities, even though the curative properties of the waters were not recognized before the Romans came. Water deities, indeed, both male and female, seem to have been the most widely worshipped of all Celtic deities—a not surprising thing when one considers the life-giving properties of water, its indispensability.   There was probably another sacred spring, like that at Bath, at Buxton; the Romans discovered the curative properties of that too, and built the town of Aquae Arnemetiae—Arnemetia 'who dwelt over against the sacred grove'—and resorted to it as they did to Bath.   But no temple of their building has been excavated there in honour of Arnemetia though one may have existed.   A description has already been given of the nymph of the sacred spring hidden in the 'Deep Room' at Lullingstone; examples could be multiplied.   We might also under this head include another god localized at Lydney in Gloucestershire, whose Celtic name is found nowhere else (this need not mean that he was not worshipped anywhere else).   This was Nodens, or Nudens, the hunter-god of the

Forest of Dean, as we may deduce from the frequency of representations of hounds found in his sanctuary. But to judge by tokens hung up there he too was also a water-deity. Nodens, however, is a specially interesting case and we shall say more about him in a more suitable context presently.

In all, we have about forty names of Celtic deities, most of them representing localized cults; but there must have been many more which have left behind no tangible traces. The remote valleys and mountains of Wales, for instance, must have been full of gods and goddesses, even if only vague spirits of place, the *genii loci* as the Romans, who had their own such, called them, of which we know nothing, not even their names.

We shall now never know how many sanctuaries and shrines, how many sacred places of wood and stream and hilltop dotted the countryside in those long past centuries. Sometimes, however, we may get a glimmering of the truth when we light upon a St. Felix's Well, St. Agnes's Spring, St. John's Grotto. Nearly all such places are Christianized versions of ancient Celtic cults centring upon some beneficent natural feature; a Christian saint has taken over in them the powers once ascribed to the demoted god.

Round some of the ancient sanctuaries the people would have gathered in the Roman era to trade and barter, because it was thought that the presence of the deity would hallow their transactions, and the sacred peace which the god brought to the place would be potent in preventing brawls and disputes over merchandise. Entertainments would be provided for the throngs gathered there; the assembly would partake of the nature of the later mediaeval fair. As Mercury was the Roman god of commerce and trading, he would be invoked with the native deity of the fairground, but not alone. He would be associated with the Celtic Rosmerta.

Other pre-Roman holy places would keep their ancient deities untouched by romanization. Originally the Celts worshipped the invisible forces of nature in the open air; their 'temples' were sacred trees and standing stones which were considered as the dwelling-places of the god. But now, having been taught by the Romans how to build more

substantially than heretofore, the Britons would erect
temples for the god or gods of the place, wherein the deity
might dwell, and where his devotees might hang up their
votive offerings—miniature bronze axes, small bronze birds
and plaques or any other token emblematic of the deity's
powers.

Had we journeyed the roads of Roman Britain long ago
we should have come upon these little temples and lesser
wayside shrines as often as the traveller in Roman Catholic
lands today comes upon wayside Calvaries and crosses.
They must have been a feature as frequent and as familiar as
the towers of parish churches of the present time. On the
North and South Downs, on heaths beside the Roman roads,
at hunters' meeting-places, by springs and watersmeets, at
the sources of rivers and on lonely moors, and in the sacred
groves which the Celts called *nemeton*, the holy places of the
woods, they would have been found. We know this
because in the sixth century, long after the *pax Romana* was
no more and Roman dominion in Britain was a faded
memory of the ashes of a past glory, the querulous monk
Gildas wailed in Jeremiah-like lamentation about the 'ruins
of [pagan] shrines everywhere, their walls, inside and out,
bristling with weathered idols of savage mien'. So he describes the temples and sanctuaries of Mars Alator, Toutates,
Ialonus god of the meadows, and others whose names in his
day had sunk into greater oblivion even than their temples
have done in ours.

Gildas was a Welshman, and was doubtless describing the
more remote sanctuaries on the borders of Wales. In less
isolated areas the temples would be more architectural. But
we must not imagine them looking like small versions of the
Parthenon at Athens, the temple of Fortuna Virilis at Rome,
or even the Maison Carrée at Nîmes. There may have been
a fair number of temples of classical type in Britain, but we
are certain of only five: at Bath, Colchester, Verulamium,
Wroxeter and Corbridge—all towns where for one reason or
another Roman influence was strong. There may have
been a few more: at Buxton, Lincoln and Caerwent, with two
or three others perhaps; but of this we are not certain. The
temples of the native gods were not purely Roman at all,

nor were they purely Celtic. It has been agreed that we
should call them Romano-Celtic, and they were to be found
especially in the southern counties from Norfolk to Dorset.
Furthermore, they differed essentially from mediaeval or
later churches because they were not, like those, designed to
hold a congregation. They were nothing more than the
dwelling-place of the god, where votive offerings to him
might be made and exhibited along with the cult statue of
the god himself.

They were therefore small, rectangular buildings—there are
no round temples known in Britain, though there are a very
few polygonal ones—surrounded by a colonnade or portico,
with a pentice roof supported on dwarf columns rising from
a breast-high wall, and were lit by clerestory windows high
up above. The roofs were commonly of Roman tiles though
they might sometimes be thatched; the walls were usually of
local stone, sometimes with tile and brick quoins and
bonding courses; only rarely were they of wood. The stone
walls would be plastered externally pink or white or red;
internally they would be brightly painted in multi-coloured
horizontal bands or panels. The floors were of terracotta,
or black and white, red and white, or red and yellow
tesserae.

The square, box-like building of the temple proper was the
cella, the actual dwelling-place of the god, and home of the
cult statue if it were small enough. The portico all round
it acted as a sort of boundary between profane and holy
ground, the *cella* and the *temenos*, which was the area immediately surrounding the temple, where worshippers might
stand. Votive offerings might be displayed in the portico,
and religious processions would wind their way through it,
round the *cella*. Worshippers were admitted to the portico,
but not the *cella*, unless they were priests of the cult. They
made their vows and offered up their sacrifices in the portico,
at the altars which stood there against the temple front.

In many cases, no doubt, in the woods or by a stream or
at the meeting of two ways, the shrine would be no more than
an inscribed altar with its carved incense-cup, embowered in
ancient venerated trees and enclosed by a thicket, or by a
wattle fence. Such sanctuaries have naturally left no trace

whatever of their existence to the eyes of posterity. Here, in the holy silence broken only by the rustling of leaves, men would worship the *genius loci*, the spirit of the place whose influence they could feel around them though they could not see it, and whose protection they would seek before they continued on their way. Is not this awe in the silence of lonely places something we can feel and understand even today, seventeen and eighteen hundred years after?

We do not know the name of any god worshipped in any particular Romano-Celtic temple in Britain—for the temple of Nodens at Lydney is not a Romano-Celtic temple of the type described above at all. It is, as far as we know, unique in Britain. In the first place it is basilical—that is to say it has no outer colonnade in the classical tradition, but a nave and aisles, and thus would seem to resemble a Christian church—though this we know for certain it was not. Secondly, it has at its north-west end not a single, but a triple set of alcoves. This does not necessarily mean that three deities were venerated here, especially as no traces of altars or statues were found in them; they may have been temple treasuries, or storage places for votive offerings. Thirdly, down the long sides of the rectangular body of the temple is a series of 'chapels', each with a mosaic panel in its floor, and shut off from the 'nave' by screen walls. And lastly, it has the unusual feature of stone benches along parts of its walls, evidence of the presence of worshippers *inside* the building.

Further than this, though the temple itself stands clear of other buildings, the precinct around it is hemmed in on the north by a large building erected round a paved court-yard. This is tentatively called by modern excavators the Guest House, on the assumption that the temple was a place of pilgrimage, and had a kind of hostelry to accommodate those who journeyed to it. On the west of the precinct is a long building with a range of small rooms opening on to a verandah. We can only guess the purpose of this building. Perhaps there were shops there, selling votive offerings, as shops around the shrines of the saints did in the centres of pilgrimage in the Middle Ages. Another, quite different suggestion, more in keeping with the sanctity of the place, is that the small rooms were cubicles for sick devotees who came to Nodens as a god of healing, and slept in them the 'holy sleep' in which the god would bring them help in their sickness. It must be stressed that both these suggestions are guesswork. The actual purpose of the 'Long Building' at Lydney is another of the many things hidden from us by the accumulation of the centuries.

About the purpose of the complex of rooms adjoining the Long Building on the north there is, however, no doubt. It was a suite of baths, with hypocausts, painted walls and mosaic floors.

So we may with fair confidence conclude that Nodens was not only a god of hunting like Silvanus, as well as a water-god, as seems to be evidenced by fragments of bronze reliefs found in his temple which show fishermen, tritons, conch-shells and anchors, and a sun-god associated with fishing and the sea (for in one fragment he is represented as the Sun driving on his four-horse chariot with a *putto* on each side of him holding what appears to be a torch) but also a god of healing. The evidence lies in certain of the votive offerings hung up in his temple; it is strengthened by comparison of the temple complex with examples abroad, particularly the sanctuary of Aesculapius at Epidaurus in the Peloponnesus. To Nodens, as to Aesculapius, pilgrims resorted for cures of their physical ills, just as they were to do hundreds of years later at the shrines of the saints in the Christian Middle Ages.

Perhaps the most remarkable thing about this temple complex at Lydney is the late date in the Romano-British period of its building, for it has been proved that it could not have been built before A.D. 367. Another, more normal, late Romano-Celtic temple to a pagan deity was excavated in 1934 at Maiden Castle, the great Iron Age hill fort two miles from Dorchester in Dorset reduced by Vespasian in the early days of the conquest. For three hundred years the hilltop had been left desolate after its capture by Vespasian. Very soon after that tragedy the Romans had persuaded the remnants of the inhabitants to abandon the fort and come down to the plain where they built the town of Durnovaria for them. Then suddenly, about the year 366, this temple was built inside the deserted fort, with a house for the attendant priest, attached to it. Why? On the Sussex Downs also, on Chanctonbury, where the eighteenth-century circle of trees now grows, a landmark for miles around, there are—now buried from view—the remains of another pagan temple of about the same date. What was the reason for this resurgence of devotion to pagan gods while the tide of Christianity was rising, even in the remote regions of Rome's most northerly province? Some have suggested that it was due to the attempts of the Emperor Julian the Apostate to rekindle the dead ashes of ancient pagan fires of sacrifice, to rebuild the fallen and neglected stones of pagan temples abandoned when Constantine made official the eastern mystery religion out of Galilee which had till then been at best despised, at worst persecuted. But though Julian had ruled as Caesar in Gaul[1] he never visited Britain, and his efforts as Augustus to revive the flickering flames of paganism in the Roman Empire were mostly exercised in the East, a long way off from Britain. In any case he did not rule long enough (he was killed in the Persian Wars in 363, having been emperor a bare three years) for his so-called reforms to strike roots, and the weakling plant withered away everywhere as soon as it had reared its head above the earth.

It seems more likely that it was the uncertain, troubled times of the second half of the fourth century, the sense of coming doom in the air that drove men back to their ancient gods, the gods who had been the stay of their more fortunate forefathers in the days of the golden age of the *Pax Romana*. And it is notable that most of these late temples were placed on hilltops; and at hilltop Lydney, and possibly at the others also, the whole temple area and its associated buildings was surrounded with a strong wall as a defence against new enemies raiding from west and south and east.

There seem to have been some elements of mysticism in the worship of Nodens, which was apparently a complex cult. Like waters rising from far off, diverse hills, each bringing down its different uprooted vegetation, but all joining at last and flowing as one, it evidently originated in

---

[1] The term 'Caesar' had at this time reverted to its former meaning of 'heir to the purple.'

several cults both native and imported, all merging in the days of the late Empire in a mysticism that was a characteristic of the religious sentiments of the time. The temple of Nodens was probably the consecrated meeting-place of a brotherhood subdivided like other mystic religions—not excluding Christianity—into various grades of initiation; and this brings us to another aspect of the religion of Roman Britain—indeed, of the Roman world of the later Empire generally—the importation, chiefly from the East, of mystery religions, of which, of course, Christianity was one.

Into Britain, probably introduced by the cosmopolitan army, came Serapis, an Egyptian corn-god and god of the harvest, connected with Osiris, god of the underworld; he is represented as an elderly deity, bearded like a Jupiter, but with a *modius*, or corn-measure, on his head. Attached to his temple were dream oracles which responded to the questionings of devotees. There came also Isis, sister of Osiris, symbolic of the creative force in Nature; and Cybele, the great Phrygian Earth Mother, another goddess of the powers of Nature, sometimes equated by the Romans with Demeter, without whom all growth on earth ceases; and Iuppiter of Doliche, whose high seat was in Commagene, and who made animal creation his footstool and the firmament of heaven his kingdom. He was said to give oracular answers to those who came to ask his advice in their perplexity, but the army considered him as a powerful war-god. The most potent of all the imported gods worshipped by the army, however—and this god was also worshipped in mercantile towns like London, where traders from many parts of the Roman Empire congregated—was the Persian god of the Unconquered Sun, Mithras (or Mithra).

Mithraism was a secret and exclusive cult. None except those who by severe preparatory ordeals both physical and mental had passed through its seven grades of initiation could comprehend its mysteries, closely guarded from all but the elect. They alone through revelation regained their original beatitude of soul and entered into union with the god (the objective of *all* mystery religions); the wicked outside communion with him were cast into the jaws of Ahriman, god of darkness—as the Christians would have called it, Hell.   Nor could anyone, except the upright and pure, those prepared to live a moral life of abstinence and self-control, showing courage, fortitude and vigilance, fidelity and constancy, hope to pass through those seven grades. The god demanded so much from his devotees that the cult of Mithraism could never be universally popular, especially as it excluded women; and the organization of its elaborate ritual required special ability likely to be found only among the commanders of the army or the well-informed and influential among the mercantile classes.   Its demands for probity in intercourse, for honourable conduct between individuals, certainly did give the cult an appeal to merchants; and undoubtedly this is the reason why the Mithraic temple, larger and of greater splendour than was usual, was built by the Wallbrook in London, where it was discovered in 1954.   The elements of that temple, excavated and moved from their original site, may still be seen in Queen Victoria Street.

This basilical temple, in plan very like early Christian churches, was evidently built and furnished at the expense of wealthy traders and perhaps the senior officers of the Cripplegate fort subsequently discovered in an angle of the Roman wall of London.   At its western end was an apse where the altar had stood, raised on a dais.   Here would have been a representation of the god slaying the sacred bull from whose blood all life flowed; probably it was in some way illuminated from behind to throw up the figure of the god in this supreme act in dramatic relief.   Pillars standing on low walls divided the central nave from the two aisles; and the place would have been dark, for the tiny clerestory openings high up in the walls would be for ventilation only.   This London temple was built entirely above ground; but Mithraic temples were often subterranean (as in some examples on Hadrian's Wall) and intentionally kept in darkness if above ground in remembrance of the fact that Mithras slew the sacred bull in a cave.   This bull-slaying symbolizes the conquest of wild Nature and the release by Mithras of vital forces from which spring the good things of the earth.   Accompanying him in his temples were the two minor gods Cautes and Cautopates, the former

with upward-pointing torch emblematic of life and the light
of day, the other with torch held down, symbolizing death
and the darkness of night. An example of a humbler
Mithraic temple at Carrawburgh on Hadrian's Wall was
excavated in the fifties of the present century. In this case
it was built, like the London temple, above ground; but part
of its interest lies in the evidence it affords of the deliberate
destruction of its trappings and images. This destruction is
paralleled in London by the apparently intentional concealment of images of pagan gods, evidently to prevent them from
being destroyed. They are a curious assortment to find in a
temple of Mithras—Minerva, Hermes, Serapis and a Bacchus
group which included the drunken Silenus riding as usual
on a donkey, and accompanied as usual by a satyr; but they
all have some connection with the underworld, like Mithras
himself, and this may explain their presence. It seems
almost certain that in both cases iconoclastic Christians are
the cause of the destruction on the one hand, the protecting
concealment on the other. The Christians were infuriated
by Mithraism, because they thought they saw a mocking
travesty of Christian beliefs and sacraments in its story of
the shepherds who witnessed the miracle of the birth of the
god from the rock and worshipped him; in its use of water or
blood in a kind of baptism, with the sealing of initiates upon
the forehead with the mark of their calling; its idea of communion with the god through a sacramental meal and a
communion service commemorating the last meal which
Helios and Mithras partook of together on earth, and in its
promise of resurrection after death.

This desire for some more emotional belief than that which
the old gods offered, this idea that permeated the mysteries
that the divine and immortal soul of man could be purified
of its grosser elements by moral discipline, by mystical
ecstacy attained through special ritual and the possession
of secret spiritual knowledge, and that the purification
would culminate in the soul's union with the deity and a
temporary foretaste on this earth of eternal union with him
in a life to come, is a phenomenon of the later Roman
Empire, though it had begun to manifest itself much earlier,
even during the first century of our era. Far away in

Pompeii, which was destroyed in A.D. 79, we have painted on
the walls in a room of the 'Villa of the Mysteries' a panorama
of the mystic union of a woman initiate with the ecstatic
Dionysus (the Roman Bacchus); we have an account by
Apuleius, who wrote his *Golden Ass* round about the middle
of the second century A.D. of the soul's satisfaction which
comes from the mystical union through secret rites with Isis,
'the supreme deity of the thousand names', who greets her
novice with the words, 'Lo, I come to thee, the parent of all
nature, the highest of holy spirits, whose godhead the whole
world worships.' The time was ripe, when Jesus of Naza-
reth appeared in the pagan world, for a religion which
promised to all men and women, rich and poor alike, slave
and free, comfort for the individual soul and eternal life
after death in the presence of the Godhead. The old religions could not offer this; with the exception of Mithraism,
they could not, as Christianity did, promise recompense in
the hereafter for the tribulations of this world, or reward
after death for a life well lived. Intelligent and educated
Romans in the days of Cicero, Seneca, Boethius and
Marcus Aurelius had turned to philosophy when the
sterile official worship of the Roman state could no longer
be taken seriously by them or offer any acceptable answer
to the great riddle of the purpose of life; but all men had not
the training or the education to understand and find
comfort in philosophy. To those who did not have it
Christianity came as a lantern bringing light in the complexity of tortuous ways winding inexorably to the dark
bourne of death; and they eagerly followed its guiding
light.

We do not know how or when Christianity first came to
Britain. Several picturesque legends on the subject exist,
all of them without foundation in fact. The best known is
that Joseph of Arimathea, chosen as a missionary to our
land by St. Philip, brought the worship of Christ from Gaul,
leaving his home and all he had, but bringing with him not
his poverty alone, but the precious relic, in two ampullae,
of the Blood of Christ. The pagan king Arviragus rejected
his teaching, but gave him a place of sojourn on an island
in the marshes among the lake dwellings of Meare called

Yniswitrin—the Glass Isle, now called Glastonbury. There, at the foot of the Tor, Joseph thrust his pilgrim staff into the ground. Straightway it budded and flourished; and though the original 'Holy Thorn' was uprooted by the Puritans long after, a slip of it was saved, which 'still blooms at Christmas, mindful of our Lord'. The old legend goes on to say that this man of Arimathea, who had given up his own sepulchre to receive the body of Christ in the Holy Land, sleeps his last sleep in the shadow of the little oratory 'of twisted twigs'—that is, of wattle—which he had built in Avalon.

This is one of those legends which we very much wish we could believe; but the only part of it which is likely to be true is that at the foot of Tor Hill at Glastonbury was built the first Christian church in Britain—though of that church nothing whatever remains. Nor is it likely that it was built as early as A.D. 63, the date given for St. Joseph's journey to Britain. Nevertheless, it does seem that Christianity had established itself in some parts of Britain as early as the second century.

By the early fourth century we are on firmer ground. There almost certainly was an Albanus of Verulamium who was martyred during the persecution of the Christians by Diocletian in the opening years of that century, though St. Alban, whose abbey was built in Norman days largely of Roman bricks from the ruins of Verulamium, was probably not, as Bede says, a soldier, but an ordinary British inhabitant of that town.

A few years after his martyrdom three bishops representing British communities attended the Council of Arles in 314. By this time the Edict of Milan, granting toleration to the Christians, had been issued by Constantine the Great (in 313) and the new faith had emerged into the light and was publicly organizing itself. The Christian community in Britain in these earlier days appears, however, to have been poor, without the patronage of wealthy men. This may partly explain the paucity of material remains of the faith turned up today by the spades of archaeologists. At this date the Christians were possibly too poor to build churches of any material more substantial than wattle and daub or timber—which would, after a few decades, leave little trace in the earth.

We have the negative evidence of the destruction of Mithraic temples, presumably by Christians. But only one certain Christian church has ever come to light—in Calleva Atrebatum (Silchester). That church, as its foundations tell us, was small, indicating (since Christianity, unlike Celtic cults, had to provide for the communal worship of congregations *inside* a church) that its worshippers were few. It was also, apparently, of late date. Christianity, it seems, was a minority religion among the people of town and country in the south; and in the army it has left no trace at all, except for the assumption that a commandant or two were the Christians who overturned the Mithraic temple at Carrawburgh and perhaps others along the line of Hadrian's Wall.

We have to remember, however, that Calleva is the only cantonal town in Britain that has ever been *completely* excavated. Other towns, beneath the sods which cover most of their earliest buildings—as at Viroconium—or beneath the mediaeval and modern buildings which cannot be moved from above antiquity, might hide the foundations of other such churches. We never know in one decade what the excavations of the next may reveal. Who would have supposed, for instance, in 1935, that beneath the quiet uplands of the Darent Valley in Kent, almost facing Lullingstone Castle, there lay buried and invisible a burnt-out Roman villa in which existed the only Christian house-church we know of in western Europe?

We have described this house-church in a previous chapter. It remains only to emphasize its importance in tracing the story of Christianity in Britain. Here, in this quiet rural valley, Christ was worshipped by countryfolk in the late fourth century even while the pagan mausoleum of some earlier owners of the villa still stood, no doubt still honoured, on the rising ground above.

It is possible that at least a few Christian churches survived in ruin in the renewed heathenism of Saxon times, and that after St. Augustine had brought Christianity back to Britain in 597 the ruins were incorporated into Saxon churches. How else shall we account for a west wall built largely of

Roman bricks, with partly Roman windows in it, and a
south-east wall similarly built, in the now much restored
church of St. Martin at Canterbury? In such ways, perhaps, traces of Romano-British Christianity may now be
hidden from us. But after taking everything into considera-
tion it has to be admitted that the proofs of Christianity in
Britain in the Roman era are meagre. There are the
foundations of one small undoubted Christian church at
Calleva; there are parts of Roman walls in the predominantly
mediaeval church of St. Martin at Canterbury, which may
or may not have been a church in the centuries before it was
brought to Bede's notice and produced his remark that there
was a church in his day (the eighth century) dedicated to
St. Martin 'built of old while the Romans were still inhabiting the land'. To this we may add a mosaic pavement or
two like those at Frampton and Hinton St. Mary, which
bear symbols seeming to indicate that those who commissioned them were Christians; the thousands of shattered
fragments of the indubitable Christian wall-paintings at
Lullingstone; the Chi-Rho monogram on a few spoons,
lamps, dishes and the like, which anyhow might have been
imported and bought by those who did not realize, or were
indifferent to, the significance of the Chi-Rho; finally there
are the references to British bishops at Church Councils on
the Continent—in one case bishops so poor that they had the
expenses of their journey paid for out of the treasury by the
Emperor Constantius, and legends, possibly true but not
authenticated, of three Christian martyrs in Britain; Alban,
Aaron and Julius of Caerleon 'which after many cruel
torments yielded their souls unto the joys of heaven' in the
Diocletian persecution of 303, as Bede tells us. And there
you have the sum total of the traces the Romano-British
Christians have left behind.

Perhaps one day the archaeologists, always digging and
trenching to disinter the buried centuries, will give us more.

XIII · THE ART OF ROMAN BRITAIN

Did native Celtic and Roman art co-exist as happily in the Romano-British era as the Celtic and Roman gods did? The answer is emphatically No.

At the outset of an account of what happened in this field it may be useful to describe the characteristics of Celtic and Roman art. We will start with the latter, as being probably more familiar and certainly more easily understood.

Some will have it that apart from architecture, in which the greatness of the Romans is freely acknowledged, there is strictly no such thing as *Roman* art, because those who produced artistic work for the Romans were all Greeks, and not Greeks of the best artistic period either, and that 'Roman' art is merely a copy, often degenerate, of Greek models. But this, like all generalization, is only a half-truth. Granted that most, if not all, of the producers of artistic work for the Romans were Greeks, granted also that much 'Roman' art is a copy of the Greek, and sometimes a degenerate copy, there are features about the work of the first centuries of our era commissioned by Romans which set it apart from even later Greek work, let alone that of the best period in the fifth century B.C. Not very much training is necessary to enable one to say whether a statue is Greek of the fifth, fourth or third centuries B.C. or 'Roman' of the days of the later Republic and the Empire. To mention only one outstanding difference: while the Greek statue will represent an ideal form, unrelated to any particular human being, the Roman will be realistic, representing a subject 'warts and all'.

In the Romano-British period a Greek artist, or one highly trained in the Greek tradition—a Gaul, perhaps—may have executed the work; but the Roman who commissioned it would state what he wanted, making the influence of his taste (or lack of it) felt, and to this extent the work would be Roman.

Two characteristics of Roman art stand out. It was, as far as the remains enable us to judge, predominantly plastic, and it was representational. Its chief manifestation was sculpture in the round or in high relief. It filled a space, it had body, solidity, rounded form; and it was a more or less accurate representation in detail of the god or goddess, man or woman, beast or bird which it sought to portray. The full light of day, as it were, shone upon its products; they cast shadows as real bodies do, they were unmistakable and at times uncompromising copies of the human or animal form. It would be rash, in the state of our limited knowledge, to say that sculpture took precedence in the classical world over painting, because statuary is more enduring than painting, and had it not been for the eruption of Vesuvius in the first century A.D. which preserved the painted rooms of Pompeii, Herculaneum and Stabiae largely intact for us we should have had little more Roman painting today than we have of Greek (and that, with the exception of painting on vases, is nothing); but it would seem that sculpture did take first place, if only because it was so often considered as an adjunct to architecture. But even in paintings, to judge from those left to us, the characteristics of plasticity and realism persist. A painted bowl of fruit, a tree or a temple, an actor in a comic mask, Mars and Venus conversing or a maiden decanting perfumes—they all have roundness and body, they all resemble what they aim at representing. They hold a mirror up to Nature and faithfully reflect the image seen there. This is classical representational art; the sort of art to which the modern world also was accustomed from the Renaissance to the later years of the nineteenth century.

Celtic art was quite different. It did not stand in the broad light of day, rounded and space-filling and lifelike. It came, it seemed, out of a shadowy dream-world. It was a remote, aloof art, linear—that is, interested in line, not body —abstract, absorbed in intricate pattern-making, to which it reduced everything, even the human form, so that it was no longer recognizable as such. Once, centuries before, when the ancestors of the native Britons who saw the coming of Julius Caesar had lived on the continent of Europe, they

WEIRD CELTIC CONVENTIONALIZATION
OF NATURAL FORM

seem to have represented in carving or metalwork strange, haunted human faces, weird birds and beasts, and tendrils of living plants which did bear some likeness to the reality; but that had been long before. By the time of the arrival of the Romans the tendrils had become linear, abstract patterns of whirling circles, the human faces had disintegrated into spirals, coils and ornamental arrangements of crescent-shaped shields (known as *peltae*); infatuation with

THE CELTIC PELTA IN A DESIGN

the beauty of curving, decorative line had banished all realism and all plasticity. It was an art as abstract and filigree-like as the design of a spider's web; a linear art of dynamic pattern, and no more.

Heavily upon this fine, introvert art descended the solid, unethereal, extrovert art of the Romans; and it crushed it out of existence—or almost so crushed it. It did linger on for a little while in the less romanized areas of the country in one medium—metalwork.

But though the impact of the Roman style crushed Celtic art it did not crush the Celtic spirit. That lived on, and vigorously enough to bring certain modifications for a while to Roman plastic art whenever it had the opportunity or will to do so. With lesser craftsmen the effort to adapt themselves to this unfamiliar, and to the Celtic spirit uncongenial form proved too much, and the artist who might have excelled in abstract patterning made an inferior bungle when he tried to work plastically and representationally. We shall see presently what happened when a more skilful artist made a similar effort.

So the brilliant and beautiful abstract art of the Celts suffered eclipse; and the pity of it was that the art which eclipsed it was, when it came to Britain, already in decline. It was not the best period of classical art which the Britons found themselves encountering; and the consequence is that with a few exceptions the existing remains of the art of the Romano-British period which we may see today in museums up and down the land are often attractive by reason of their naïveté or grotesqueness or even comic ineptitude rather than because of their artistic worth.

Leaving architecture aside for the time being, we are now, perhaps, in a position to consider the art of the Roman period in Britain as of five types. First, there is the purely classical, Graeco-Roman type, exemplified mostly in sculpture. This would all have been the work of Roman-employed Greeks or Gauls trained by them, and most of it would have been imported. Examples of it are the sculptures we mentioned in the previous chapter as being hidden from Christian iconoclasts beneath the London temple of Mithras. The benign head of Serapis with his corn-measure headdress decorated with olive-branches, the damaged but entirely classical small group of Bacchus, the drunken Silenus, a satyr and a maenad, the now helmetless head of Minerva, the seated figure of Mercury, god of profit, with small wings attached to his head and a purse in his left hand, and most important of all, the head of Mithras himself in his Phrygian cap, with eyes upturned as if looking up from his slaying of the bull—all these are of Italian marble, proof that they were imported. (The fragmentary carving of the lower part of the god's attendant, Cautopates with his lowered torch, is, however, of limestone, and the workmanship is inferior—proof of its native origin.)

In the same category fall the two marble busts of Roman dignitaries found in the 'Deep Room' at Lullingstone, and now in the British Museum, which probably represented former owners of the villa, or their relatives or ancestors; in this case the owners appear actually to have been Romans, not, as was more usual, Britons. These busts are obviously portraits, so individualistic we can deduce from them the characters of those they represented. The one was kindly, dreamy, scholarly, perhaps, and maybe a philosopher; the other was a stern leader of men, purposeful, rather grim and forbidding, a man whom his junior officers would not care to offend. These, like the Mithras groups, are of excellent classical workmanship, examples of the better work that even this period could sometimes produce.

Another example of this first type is the colossal head, twice life-size, of Constantine the Great from Eboracum, which must, of course, be a product of the early fourth century. The sculptor may have been a skilfully trained Gaul, but is more likely to have been of Mediterranean origin. We have seen that Constantine was with his father in Eboracum after Constantius Chlorus's punitive campaigns against the northern invaders, and the artist may quite likely have come to Britain with the imperial entourage. At all events it is a vigorous and realistic work, the features giving an insight into the determined character of the great emperor.

This head of Constantine is of local stone. A contrasting and much earlier female head in bronze was found, two centuries ago, in a corner of the baths at Aquae Sulis: that of Minerva, much damaged below the chin, where it was at some time broken from the body. The features and workmanship are again entirely classical; and if, as is supposed, the head (once helmeted) was cast in Gaul, it must have been in a highly romanized centre.

As an example of a full-length figure we may take a second-century bronze statuette of Mercury, not quite two feet high, which was found in the neighbourhood of Camulodunum and is now in the Colchester and Essex Museum.   This is a good example of pure classical style, no doubt imported. The arms are lost, but the stance is the familiar classical one, with the body slightly inclined to the right, the left shoulder higher than the right, the left leg slightly forward (though as the heels are raised the god was evidently originally just alighting upon something). The figure is also, in the Greek style, completely naked.

Such works as these, which are merely a few typical examples, were either executed in Britain by Mediterranean artists or else imported.   Employing as they did the most skilful craftsmen they would have been costly; and if they were commissioned by private individuals these would necessarily have been wealthy men, in most cases Britons. Many, however—like the head of Constantine—would have been destined for public places, or as cult statues of gods and goddesses donated by well-to-do natives to their favourite deities; who, in the second century, to which many of them belong, would often have been Roman ones, as we have explained in the previous chapter.

Another medium in which this pure classicism manifests itself is metal.   Scenes of classical combat are depicted on bronze helmets and face-masks for ceremonial usage; and we also find extremely ornamental designs on many jug and skillet handles.   These last often represent gods or heroes— Hercules, for instance, strangling the snakes, or Bacchus and satyrs modelled in the round; or sometimes they bear merely a mask, perhaps of Oceanus, perhaps of a lion or a dog. But one of the most famous and remarkable survivals of classical work in this medium is the fourth-century 'Mildenhall Treasure', evidently the silver dinner-service of some rich British villa owner, wealthy enough to buy or commission such imported work, who buried it in the ground during the troubles in the twilight of Roman Britain— perhaps when he foresaw some Saxon raid in the opening years of the fifth century—and never returned to retrieve his treasure.   Mildenhall, where the hoard was found, is in Suffolk, an area that lay open to the Saxon menace.   (A similar treasure of silver, of about the same date, was evidently looted and carried off by raiders beyond the boundaries of the province, to be discovered in recent times at Traprain Law, East Lothian.)

We have no space here to describe the whirling, dancing patterns on all the platters, flanged and scalloped bowls, spoons, and ladle-handles of the Mildenhall Treasure. We may, however, say a few words about the most outstanding piece in the hoard. This is a large round dish with a beaded rim, perfectly preserved and covered with reliefs of naked nereids and sea-centaurs twisting round a mask of Oceanus staring wildly out at us, his cheeks and nostrils distended, from the centre of the dish. Seaweed forms his beard; four dolphins leap from his 'handle-bar' moustache and disordered hair. Outside the circle of shells enclosing this scene is a broad, flowing frieze of Bacchus with his foot on a panther and holding a thyrsus and bunch of grapes. Silenus is near by, offering his wine-cup and Hercules, drunken, is upheld by two obliging satyrs. Maenads, satyrs and a bearded Pan with pan-pipes all join in the revel rout, the robes and loosely bound hair of the maenads windily twist and twirl, the naked males leap in a wild, ecstatic dance.

Classical features in pottery are exemplified by the mass-produced 'Samian' ware which still exists in monotonous profusion in nearly every museum of antiquities in the country. This highly glazed red ware from Gaul, stamped in relief from dies with figures of animals, hunting scenes, dancing men and maidens and floral scrolls, ousted the pre-Roman Celtic pottery. But in the second century the Gallic potteries closed down, and the importing of Samian ware ceased. What took its place we will describe presently.

Something has already been said in a previous chapter about the place of paintings and mosaics in house-decoration; here we need only say that with only a few exceptions those who designed and those who executed them were artists from Mediterranean lands, and that they therefore fall into this first group which we have been describing. There is nothing Celtic about them; they represent commissions from rich patrons adopting Roman fashions who could afford, and were satisfied with, the services of classically trained craftsmen from abroad.

Let us now turn to the second type of artistic work to be

found in Roman Britain: that which shows a fusion of
classical and Celtic workmanship, produced by an imagina-
tive and skilled native artist copying the classical style but
asserting his own individuality while he did so.

Such examples as we have of this type are often remarkable
—arresting and vital. The best of them compare with the
academic, polished efficiency of classical products as a rugged
landscape of mountain and forest compares with a municipal
park where 'tulips grow as they are told' and all the lawns
are neatly mown. The outstanding example is the Medusa

RECONSTRUCTION OF THE PEDIMENT OF THE TEMPLE OF SULIS
MINERVA AT AQUAE SULIS (BATH)

head in local Bath stone which was carved to form the
centre-piece of the shield in the pediment of the classical
temple of Sulis Minerva at Bath. There are enough fragments remaining from this pediment to enable us to judge
that, like the temple itself, its scheme was entirely classical,
with Victories standing on globes upholding the shield, and
Tritons blowing conch-shells in the lower corners. Classical
also is the idea of a Medusa-head in a central shield. Even
the representation of Medusa as male, with beard and
moustache among her snaky locks, is not entirely unknown
in the Roman world when sea-Medusas and water deities
are represented.

But the technique of this Medusa is not classical. Strictly
speaking it is not sculpture at all—that is to say it is not
plastic, it does not stand out from the flat surface from which
it is carved. It is two-dimensional, a graphic, linear design,
an engraving (as it has been called) on a disc. Here
obviously we have the Celt at work—whether Gaul or Briton
is not established—the lover of curving line, of decorative

K

pattern making a play of light and shade; both execution and spirit are Celtic. This filling of a space with rich ornament of high decorative quality was something alien to the classical artist. We have only to look at the remains of the sculptures of the pediments of the Parthenon to see how a Greek treated spatial filling.

Sometimes, however, perhaps in emulation of classical work which he admired, a native artist—in this case definitely a Briton, working on British limestone—did produce something more sculptural—something in the round. The first-century small head of a man found at Gloucester is what he produced. This is classically three-dimensional, classically representational; it could even have been a likeness of someone the artist knew. Quite plainly some piece of Roman portrait statuary inspired it. But the Celtic spirit breaks through the classical shell. There is a strange, other-worldly atmosphere about this aloof and dreaming youth with the oval, tapering face, huge bulging eyeballs, straight, narrow nose and slit-like mouth above a beardless chin; and the locks of his hair form a Celtic pattern of grooved lines above his brow.

Another Celtic artist, influenced perhaps by some Roman funeral monument, a little later produced his version of a sculptured head. This is the neckless visage of an under-world goddess found at Towcester in Northamptonshire, its chin resting directly on a low base, a not unusual feature of funerary sculpture. The modelling of this face is nearer to the classical norm than that just described. But it has the same conventionally patterned hair, the same large, bulging eyes, the same wedge-like nose. Here, however, the eyes are deeply drilled so that they stare fiercely; and the slit-like mouth is bent like a bow in woeful discontent emphasized by the goddess's puckered brows. There is something almost frightening in the aspect of this unearthly goddess. The Celtic dream-world lies behind this manifestation of infernal powers. No Roman, still less Greek, could have evolved such an image of an underworld deity.

Different again, yet still showing the Celtic spirit emerging from the classical form is the second-century statue of a reclining river-god found in the baths of the commandant's

house at Cilurnum (Chesters) on Hadrian's Wall. The
figure is bearded and half draped and leans with his left
elbow upon the huge mask of a water deity—perhaps a
personification of Oceanus, into which the North Tyne, the
river which gave water for the baths at Cilurnum, eventually
flows. This type of mask, the attitude of the god who leans
upon it and the sculptural, three-dimensional treatment of
the figure are all classical. But Celtic is the decorative
treatment of the drapery. It falls from the god's left
shoulder in the characteristic Celtic spiral curve, and across
his knees it lies in a series of patterned ridges. No classically
trained sculptor would ever have carved drapery so linearly
patterned as this, making ornament an outstanding feature
in its own right.

The head of another bearded river-god, also probably
second century, from Cirencester, shows the same classical
plasticity, but is modelled with a rude, vigorous strength as
if hacked out of the stone rather than chiselled. Its masterful
lines powerfully suggest the tumultuous potency of the god of
oceans and all waters.

In these examples the classical and Celtic elements are
about evenly distributed. But occasionally the Celtic
impulse rose so strongly in the carver that though he adopted
a classical mould for his work every detail of what he
produced was inspired by Celticism, so that the finished
product was predominantly Celtic. Such a work is the head
of a Celtic god to be seen in the Tullie House Museum at
Carlisle, where under the grimly scowling brows the eyes
are gouged out into deep, shadowy hollows, the nose is a
broken wedge shape, the cruel, remorseless mouth is nothing
but a rectangular slot, and the cheeks are so hacked out that
they are like half-finished cubes, not rounded cheeks at all.
This is an angry god whom no devotee would dare to offend.
His very glance chills with awe and fear, around him stirs
a shuddering aura of the supernatural. Is this a Celt's
version of the classical Jupiter Ammon, since there are
curling ram's horns behind his ears?

This eerie unworldliness in Celtic art is something that no
Roman sculptor ever encompasses.

Two further examples, one of animal sculpture, one of a

tombstone, will be enough to illustrate this fusion of Roman and Celtic in the hands of the more gifted Celtic artists.

The animal sculpture represents a lion devouring a stag, and it comes from Corbridge, the one-time supply depôt for Hadrian's Wall. It may originally have been a tomb monument, but was later adapted as a fountain. Here again the subject and the modelling are classically three-dimensional; but the head of the despoiler is more human than leonine, and neither the beast's paws nor his stylized mane is classically realistic. Even the proportions of the lion are not entirely accurate. This is a vital, vigorous version of a classical theme, but too vital, too brutally vigorous for any Graeco-Roman hand of empire days to have produced it.

TOMBSTONE OF A LADY, IN THE TULLIE HOUSE
MUSEUM, CARLISLE

The tombstone is one of the more attractive exhibits in the Tullie House Museum. Here once again, although classical influence is strong in the design of the two tomb-figures, Celtic features tend to outweigh the classical. The attraction of this piece lies not in its hackneyed portrayal of a mother seated under a coved niche caressing the little child at her knee who is fondling a bird in her mother's lap, but in the pattern of deeply cut, almost parallel lines which produce a striking effect, enhanced by the radiating grooves in the wheel-shaped fan in the lady's hand, of black and white design, of light and shade—the very things that most appealed to the Celtic mind. In the satisfaction they give us we forget to notice that the proportions of both figures are such as no purely classical artist would have allowed for a moment. But the Celt was fascinated by his pattern of decorative lines; the proportions of his figures were of only secondary importance to him.

And now a word about the pottery which came upon the market when the supply of Samian failed. This was what is known as Castor ware, and it too was an imitation of the classical, though with a difference, like the sculptural works we have been discussing. Obviously the patterns on them—chiefly of animal groups, hunting scenes and floral scrolls—are derived from the reliefs on Samian; but no one can fail to distinguish between Samian and Castor. The shapes are different, for Castor reverts to the old, pre-Roman types; Samian has a hard, high red glaze, Castor a dull, dark brown or black one; and the method of applying the pattern is different. On Samian ware it was stamped from dies, and is consequently of one colour with the bowl; on Castor it was barbotine—that is, white wet clay squeezed through a funnel on to the vessel before it was fired, very much as confectioners today squeeze a pattern of icing sugar on to a cake. Most important of all, the decorative scenes represented on Castor ware are but an imitation of those on Samian, yet they are imbued—as the sculptures we have been describing are imbued—with the dynamic Celtic spirit. The tame and frigid Samian hunting scenes become on Castor ware energetic and vital. Hounds strain forward with open jaws and protruding tongues, hunted hares leap for their lives, ears lain backward, over the swirling, curvilinear lines of tendrils and plants. Of course the scenes are stereotyped, repeated *ad nauseam* on vessel after vessel; but at least they show that even in this humblest of the arts the Roman spirit, though it tended to dominate it, had not yet extinguished the Celtic.

It is significant that, if we except pottery, all the foregoing examples of the successful fusion of classical and Celtic characteristics are of the second, or at latest the early third century. In this earlier period of the Roman occupation certain gifted Celtic artists, beholding classical sculpture, were inspired to use its forms while infusing into them their own alien spirit, their own tendency towards decorative pattern, the linear design, the sweeping curve, the other-worldly, eerie or haunting quality that gave their products such vitality. Only the former love of the pure abstract was missing from their Celticism: that had already, forever, been crushed by the weight of Roman art. Had the work of such artists continued to be produced then there might have arisen a real, fruitful Romano-Celtic school which would have brought forth original work of lasting merit.

But for some reason the marriage of Roman and Celtic art did not last. Why it did not we can only conjecture. Perhaps the classical hand lay too heavily upon the artists; perhaps the taste of patrons degenerated, so that such artists were not encouraged; perhaps, as the years went by, the native Britons forgot their former pre-conquest skill in the manipulation of abstract pattern; perhaps the Celtic style needed the fresh, bracing air of independence, free of the smooth veneer of classical civilization to nourish it, and when their lives, protected by the bulwark of the Roman frontier armies, became comfortable, sheltered, easy and even luxurious, that half barbaric flower drooped and died. The fact remains that after the early part of the third century we come to the third type of art in Roman Britain: that executed by craftsmen of little skill doing their best to copy classical models without having adequate knowledge of the principles which guided it, or else destitute of the ability even to imitate it exactly.

Of this type there are many examples. Typical is the statuette of a Genius in the Tullie House Museum. This, like the more skilful examples mentioned above, copied a

A GENIUS

The classical conception of a genius with
dish and cornucopia is followed, but the
grotesque proportions, clumsy hands and
enormous head show native work of an
inferior artist

Graeco-Roman art-type with its figure half draped holding
a sacrificial *patera* in the right hand and a horn of plenty in
the left, and wearing a mural crown, and retained the
Celtic characteristics of drapery patterned with deeply
incised parallel lines. But here the proportions of the
figure are ludicrous. The head and left hand are far too
huge for the body, which is that of a shapeless dwarf with
tiny feet; and the Celtic patterning on the garments is halting,
scrappy, quite destitute of the Celtic flowing grace. The

whole effect is wooden and lifeless; the figure's only charm is its childlike naïveté.

The relief of Hercules killing the hydra which may be seen in the museum at Corstopitum is perhaps more clumsy than inept. The native artist was here trying to render in Graeco-Roman style a classical legend, but simply had not the technical skill to manage his material.

A similar criticism may be offered of the triptych found at Carrawburgh in Coventina's well, just outside the fort of Brocolitia, on Hadrian's Wall. Beneath each of the three classical-style columned niches reclines (if that is the right word; wafts in the air would perhaps be a better description) a water-nymph derived from some classical copybook by a British artist unequal both to the task of correctly imitating the classical prototype and of investing his figures with the

MOSAIC OF THE SHE-WOLF AND ROMULUS AND
REMUS (DEBASED CLASSICAL STYLE)

Celtic spirit. In trying, for instance, to copy the falling folds of drapery of a classical figure he has lost the capacity of investing them with the dynamic curving line and arresting verve of the Celtic urge towards decorative pattern.

Even more clumsy and ungainly is the relief from Bremenium (High Rochester in Northumberland) of three female figures, one apparently bathing, the others bearing vessels for the bath.   This may be a portrayal of Venus with her attendants, or three water-nymphs again; but if the central figure is indeed Venus no Greek or Roman could possibly have recognized in this ugly female the goddess of love and beauty, Aphrodite born of the foam of the sea. She more resembles a newt, or the caricature of a frog.

The fourth type of Romano-British art need not detain us long.   It consists in the humble votive offerings made for sale to poorer patrons who could not afford skilled work, and for all we know did not even appreciate it.   Small pipeclay images of gods and goddesses, or miniature, roughly made versions of animals and birds, make up the sum.   They hardly rank as art at all; indeed, some of them were probably no more than the children's toys.

In the fifth category we place the only purely Celtic art that lasted for a little while after the Roman conquest—the abstract patterning on objects of metal—the shapes of which objects were often Roman, but their decoration was unmistakably Celtic.   Especially are we concerned here with

ABSTRACT CELTIC PATTERN OF CURVING LINES

brooches, where traditions of Celtic metalwork lingered on when they had disappeared from larger objects. Brooches in those days were not, as they mostly are today, worn for ornament.   They were used to fasten clothes, especially to hold cloaks in place on the shoulder or at the neck.   They were therefore objects of utility; but the real

Celtic spirit shines forth in the care which was taken to make them also objects of beauty.   In the incised flowing lines, the swelling trumpet patterns, the crescent-shaped decorative form known as the *pelta*, and the whirling triskele (a device of three curving shapes joined at a centre from which they wheel around) the craftsmen also set pastes of coloured enamel to enhance the brooches' charm.

THE CELTIC 'TRISKELE'

We often forget, as we look at the age-dimmed remnants of these past centuries, that chromatic gaiety once irradiated them; that to our more muted modern tastes they would even have appeared gaudy in their pristine splendour.   One type of brooch—the 'dragonesque'—it is something like a little twisting sea-horse—did not owe even its shape to Roman influence; it is a purely Celtic form.

These Celtic brooches mostly flourished in the north— that is, the least romanized part of the province; but sad to say even there they seem to have died out after the close of the second century.

To conclude this chapter we will briefly mention architecture in Roman Britain; briefly, although it was the greatest art-form of the Roman world, because outside strictly utilitarian military buildings and defensive works like town walls, practically nothing remains of the grandeur that was Roman architecture in this country.   The natives of Britain at the time of the Roman conquest had no architecture, so in this field Roman methods held undisputed sway.   But of all their temples, theatres and amphitheatres, fora, thermae, basilicae, triumphal arches and palaces,

which must have made majestic the cities of Britain, hardly
anything now remains.   There are the half effaced ruins of
a theatre at Verulamium; the lower walls and an entrance
arch or two with part of a staircase of a military amphitheatre at Isca (Caerleon); a gateway of old Corstopitum
removed bodily and set up as the western tower-arch in
Corbridge church; fragmentary slabs of the pediment of the
temple of Sulis Minerva at Aquae Sulis; the foundations and
mosaic floors (which are hardly architecture) of a vast,
vanished palace at Fishbourne near Chichester; and broken
columns here and there, monolithic and otherwise, in certain
museums, and that is about all.   If we had no knowledge
of Roman architecture from its remains elsewhere in Europe,
Asia and Africa, these pitifully meagre relics would give us
but a poor idea of its former majesty and grandeur.

It is useless to go seeking in Britain for the vanished glory
of Roman architecture.   The best we can do is to stand in
imagination beside that wandering Saxon poet from among
the invaders who thought of it as 'the work of giants', who
saw it twelve hundred or more years ago, before it had
crumbled back entirely into the earth on which it had stood,
and filled with melancholy for the wonders of the past which
he hardly understood, wrote a poem which has in part come
down to us:

> Bright were the castle dwellings, many the bath-houses,
> lofty the crowding pinnacles, loud the uproar of men therein
> till Fate the mighty cast all down . . . these courtyards and these
> high gateways are decaying; the timbers of the roofs are
> stripped of their tiles, the roofs of the dwelling-places where in
> days gone by men in their multitudes gazed on the treasures of
> silver and jewels . . . here once stood stone courtyards; here the
> gushing stream sprang forth all hot; and within its glorious
> circuit the wall enclosed everything . . . spacious was it all
> then. . . .

XIV · THE GREAT INVASION

We left the people of Britain, particularly the villa-owners of the countryside, enjoying a period of peace and prosperity from the accession of Constantine the Great to the middle of the fourth century. But these halcyon days were to prove the stillness and hush which often precedes a violent storm. Already in the reign of Constans, the youngest of Constantine's sons, who ruled over the West from 340 to 350,[1] the Picts had made a sudden attack in the north, on the districts adjacent to Hadrian's Wall, and there had been a sinister feature to their attack. They had been aided and abetted in it by barbarian allies referred to by the Roman historians as Scotti. These marauders were originally, it seems, a tribe from north-west Ireland, who were destined to become the scourge of the western coasts of Britain, from the Solway Firth to the Bristol Channel, and whose depredations and destructive forays, increasing in intensity through the years, were to last for nearly a century. Like the destructive exploits of the Vikings four hundred years after, their first attacks, led by hardy adventurers of no particular standing, were to be sporadic and tentative; later they were to develop in extent and force, when not merely tribal chieftains, but even High Kings of Ireland were to lead them.

Even this first combined raid of the Picti and Scotti was serious enough to bring Constans in person to Britain when the report reached him that Hadrian's Wall had yet again been overrun in several places. He did, however, manage to patch up peace, and to restore and re-garrison the Wall.

But there was trouble again in the same quarter when his brother Constantius was ruling the Roman Empire alone; and from 360 onwards, as the storm clouds gathered more ominously and the thunder rolled more loudly, the raids

[1] Constantius II, another son of Constantine, ruled the East till 350; then eliminated his brother Constans and ruled the whole Empire till 361.

of the Picts and Scots intensified. Julian, Constantius's cousin, then ruling as Caesar in Gaul, sent over some auxiliaries to cope with the situation. (Britain, it will be remembered, was part of the Praefecture of Gaul, and its safety was the Caesar's responsibility.) But when, on the death of Constantius, Julian in his turn became emperor, we hear no more for a little while of what was happening in Britain. The matters which interested the writers of the three years 361–3 were not the raids of the Picts and Scots and the woes of the northern part of the diocese of Britain, but Julian the Apostate's struggle to arrest the spread of Christianity, and his wars against the Persians.

But after he had died in the East in those wars, and Valentinian I was reigning in the West, we hear in 366 of renewed rumblings of the approaching storm, rumblings louder than before, for now, for the first time since the days, long past, of the admiral Carausius, the Saxons had appeared again off the eastern coasts. And not only that. A fourth enemy had materialized out of the west: 'a warlike race of men', referred to as Attacotti. Who these 'Attacotti' were is not certain, nor even if their name has come down to us correctly. Probably they were another Irish tribe in a low state of civilization; or perhaps not a tribe so much as a band of barbaric pirates from the district around Ath-Cliath (from which their name, latinized, may have been derived) a place which the Vikings were later to call Dublin. But more important than their origin is the fact of their adhesion to the plundering hordes which at last, acting deliberately in unison (an unusual state of affairs with barbarians) moved in on Britain from north and west and east simultaneously in the worst invasion that Britain had ever suffered during the Roman occupation, and broke like an engulfing flood upon the land. This was in 367.

In the north the Picts crashed through Hadrian's Wall and poured over Brigantia. Fullofaudes, a romanized Frank, that is, of formerly barbaric Teutonic stock, the *Dux Britanniarum*, commander of the northern forces, the legions at York and Chester and the auxiliaries along Hadrian's Wall, fell into an ambush and perished. Thereupon, now leaderless, though some undefeated units of the Sixth and

Twentieth legions undoubtedly stayed at their posts, many
of them and most of the auxiliaries disbanded themselves
in panic, or fought isolated ineffective actions in bands
scattered here, there and everywhere. In the south,
Nectaridus, the *Comes Litoris Saxonici*, making ready to fight
independently of the Northern Command against attacking
Saxon fleets, was defeated, and since no more was ever
heard of him was presumably killed. The Irish, including
doubtless the Attacotti, meanwhile fell upon the west.

The defences of the diocese were shattered; and from north,
west and east the invaders poured unchecked over the island,
looting, destroying, sacking and murdering as they moved
onwards. They came down even to the prosperous south,
which had not heard the sound of war for centuries; and
though the larger towns, which were either walled or whose
citizens hastily flung up walls as speedily as they might,
escaped all disasters except famine and epidemic as refugees
flocked in from the undefended countryside, the villa farms
and estates, defenceless as they were in the hands of unmili-
tary proprietors innocent of any skill in repelling invaders,
must have gone up in flames one after the other. They had
been built for comfort, not for war, and were of less avail
against enemies than the old ancestral 'duns' of British
chieftains of pre-Roman days would have been.

The army of Britain was now broken up and completely
useless. How many smaller forts besides those of Hadrian's
Wall and those of the Saxon Shore were overrun and sacked
in these disastrous weeks, how many of their defenders were
slain, what were the fates of those soldiers and civilians who
offered resistance to the invaders, we shall now never know.
The legions, or what was left of them, were apparently
immobilized, and with the enemy surging like a tempestuous
sea over all the land that lay between them, to act in accordance with a general plan was impossible. Civil administration as well as military was at a standstill. To north
and south soldiers and civilians alike were completely
demoralized. The countryside was overrun with panic-
stricken refugees, and isolated bodies of troops, themselves
in desperate need, turned plunderers.

The Emperor Valentinian, returning from hurling back

across the Rhine the Alemanni who had crossed that river and wasted the Roman lands on its western bank, was greeted by this news from Britain as he was travelling from Ambiani to Treveri (Amiens to Trier). It was enough to make a stronger leader than Valentinian lose his head, and for a while the emperor's actions seem to have been governed by horror-stricken impulse rather than by reason. The officials he sent to Britain to investigate effected nothing; and the year 368 had come before he recovered his wits sufficiently to choose the best man for the crisis. This was a Spaniard, Count Theodosius, called the 'Elder' to distinguish him from his more famous son of the same name who comes into history as emperor of the East some years later. Him Valentinian sent to Britain as commander-in-chief, promising that reinforcements from the best forces at his disposal would follow him immediately to retrieve the disastrous situation in Britain.

There can be no doubt that the emperor chose his man well. Theodosius was not only an experienced, but a judicious and skilled commander; one, moreover, of outstanding personality and unimpeachable character. He landed at Rutupiae on Thanet without opposition, for no doubt his naval escort was strong enough to intimidate the pirate craft which must have been infesting the seas between Gaul and Britain. But after landing he found that matters were in a worse plight than he had foreseen. Probably he had imagined that he would be able to collect a force out of the wrecks of the provincial army which, with the reinforcements following him, would be sufficient to enable him to advance against the enemy; but he soon realized that this was a vain hope. He had intended making London his base, for London was still holding out behind its walls, though the lands all round it were swarming with foes— chiefly Saxons, in this area, with, possibly, a few Irish. But he found he could not at present do this. He had to wait till the reinforcements promised by the emperor arrived. Valentinian, a less than worthy emperor in most respects, does at least seem to have estimated correctly the character and ability of Theodosius, and to have trusted him implicitly; and when made aware of the seriousness and difficulty of the situation in Britain he gave his general the best soldiers he could muster, as he was soon to give the additional help he asked for to further the execution of his plans.

As soon as the leading regiments of the reinforcements had arrived Theodosius began advancing on a wide front towards London. The invaders, who until now had had everything their own way, were taken by surprise in their reckless self-confidence. Their resistance to Theodosius's army was clogged by the plunder they were carrying, the stolen flocks and herds they were driving before them, and the crowds of prisoners they were dragging along with them. As the commander-in-chief's avenging soldiers fell upon them the marauders, disordered, disunited, straggling as they were, gave way, one band of them after another. In an incredibly short time the country round London was swept clear. Plunder was recovered and prisoners freed, and Theodosius entered harassed London in triumph.

The captives were restored to their homes—which they had certainly believed they would never see again—and as far as was possible the plunder rescued from the invaders was returned to its rightful owners. Of some of the loot there were no claimants left alive, for they had died in vain defence of their property. This the general distributed to his soldiers as a gratuity for their unwearying and praiseworthy efforts in this initial operation against the enemy.

This done, Theodosius next considered how he might embark upon the main and most difficult part of his task— the reconquest of the whole country north of the Thames and up to Hadrian's Wall, and the reestablishment of order and the civil government.

Knowing that he must have help in this gigantic enterprise, Theodosius requested it from the emperor. He asked for the administrator Civilis to be sent to him to aid him in the restoration of civil government, and a certain Dulcitius to be his second-in-command in the military sphere. These men were without delay despatched to Britain by Valentinian.

Theodosius's next step was to strengthen his armed forces. To save what he could of the wreck of the army of the diocese he proclaimed immunity to all deserters who should return to their units, and any self-disbanded remnants straggling

about the countryside, for he evidently did not consider
them all as wilful deserters but victims of circumstance.
This proclamation had the desired effect.   Soon the former
deserters flocking to London were joined by others who had
been perseveringly but ineffectively carrying on lone resistance in isolated units against the enemy.   All these, during
the winter of 368–9, Theodosius reorganized into an effective
army.   It seems very probable that at the same time he
prepared some sort of efficient fleet and restored the civil
administration.   He even established a mint so that prompt
pay would be forthcoming for the army—an additional
incentive to discipline.   Then, when all was ready, his army
thoroughly trained for the arduous work that lay before it,
his fleet directed to sweep the coasts as the army pushed
forward, and, most important in the kind of warfare that he
foresaw lay ahead—a system of intelligence having been
established to facilitate the running down and destruction
of the separate bands of marauders roaming everywhere at
large over the land, the generalissimo gave the signal to
advance.

   It was uphill work fighting against such an ubiquitous and
slippery foe, but Theodosius never shrank from any of its
difficulties, and the discipline of the army, even of those
formerly panic-stricken and demoralized elements which
had lost their nerve and disbanded themselves, seems to
have been perfect—as it usually was in Roman armies, even
semi-barbarian ones like this, when they were well led.
Leaving London behind he first advanced into the Midlands.
There band after band of invaders was tracked down,
dislodged and destroyed; gradually Theodosius and the
re-formed, reinforced army of Britain began the work of
liberation.   Through the Midlands they fought their way,
and left them clear; then on they pressed over the Lincolnshire wolds, into the Yorkshire dales and across the Yorkshire
moors, where the moorland forts and military outposts which
had been either sacked by the barbarians or evacuated by
the demoralized soldiery were restored and re-garrisoned.
So at last Theodosius reached Hadrian's Wall; but he did
not stop there.   Beyond its defences he advanced up to the
Cheviot Hills, then pressed west, then even farther north.

L

'He followed the Scot with wandering sword', exclaims the panegyrist and poet Claudian, rather carried away by his enthusiasm and poetic licence, 'and clove the waters of the northern coast with his daring oars; he trod the sands of both tidal seas [that is, the Irish Sea on the west and the North Sea on the east] and the Orkney isles dripped with the blood of the routed Saxon.'

Whether Theodosius really did penetrate as far north as the Orkneys is as doubtful as the possibility that the Saxons took refuge there. What he actually did do was to establish naval squadrons to watch the western coasts against the Irish (as we may as well now call the Scotti) and to organize the system of naval defences along the Saxon Shore; he also began the building of those signal stations along the Yorkshire coast of which some remains are still visible—at Scarborough, below the mediaeval castle, for instance. His building of these outlook posts is significant. It means that this far-seeing general had realized a fact that in less than half a century was to become all too clear: that in the future danger to Britain was likely to come less and less from the north, but more and more certain to appear from the east.

So Theodosius cleared the diocese of the Britannias of the barbarous enemy, and restored it to the Roman Empire. He built the shattered Wall and re-garrisoned its larger forts —though the ruined milecastles between the forts he left unrestored and empty. He strengthened the diocese's defences, especially on that side where defences had not been needed a hundred years before—the east, the side from which the Saxons came. Thus he successfully accomplished his arduous task, and after he had returned to his master there was peace in Britain for some fifteen years. But it was not such a golden peace as it had been for fifty years before. There is little evidence that any of the burnt-out villas in the south were ever rebuilt. The confidence with which the prosperous villa-owners had lived in their indefensible and undefended villas in the open countryside, once shaken, was never restored. Most villas that are excavated today belong to a period long anterior to 360; and though evidence can be produced to show that in several places in the south still surviving villas continued to be occupied, even, in a few cases, well into the fifth century, their heyday was past. Many of the cornlands surrounding them, which had been wasted by the invaders, were never cultivated again; from the disastrous years 367 to 369 we may date the beginning of the depopulation of the countryside as many of the villa-owners and dwellers migrated to the greater security of the walled towns. But the disrupted trade of even these did not completely recover from the shock it had experienced. The Great Invasion, if not actually the beginning of the end, marks a turning-point. Henceforth the road goes downward into the mists and shadows of the valley. Within less than a hundred years night was to fall completely over that valley.

Equally melancholy is the end of the faithful general who rescued Britain from barbarian fury for a while at least, and gave the land a short respite from war. A victim of the jealousy of Valentinian's brother Valens, emperor of the East, who seems to have feared that Theodosius might make a bid for the purple, he was executed at Carthage in 376.

XV · THE BEGINNING OF THE END

When Theodosius the Elder died the emperor of the West was Gratian, the son of his old master, Valentinian I. This Gratian was, from all accounts, an amiable enough personage, not destitute of ability when he chose to bestir himself, and with some military successes to his credit against marauding Franks and Vandals. But he had certain weaknesses and objectives which made him unpopular with both the Senate in Rome and the army on the frontiers. The senators said that he neglected government for sport—he had a passion for the chase, and countered criticism with the remark, 'Did not Aeneas [the reputed founder of the Roman state] go out hunting with the Queen of Carthage?' But what angered both senators and soldiers even more, he began to show a militant spirit in combating the easy-going toleration of paganism which till his reign had been the order of the day. It is not necessary to suppose, as the army did, that in this he was as wax in the hands of Ambrosius, bishop of Milan. Ambrosius probably urged him on in dictating that 'all must worship according to the religion of the State, and that is Christianity', but the emperor would very likely have acted as he did without the bishop's prompting. The Roman senators, even at this date, still maintained paganism as the established religion; the altar of Victory which Julian the Apostate had restored to the Senate-house twenty years before still stood there, and the ancient pagan ceremonies were still performed at the public expense. Owing to its great importance the office of Pontifex Maximus, as it had been from the days of Augustus, was still bestowed upon the emperors, even Christian ones. Gratian was the first to refuse to take this office. Ignoring the appeals of the senators he confiscated the revenues of the Roman pagan priesthoods; he overturned the altar of Victory and cast it out of the Senate-house. It is necessary for us to remember the very slight impact which Christianity had made upon the army to understand why this championship of the Christian faith made Gratian unpopular not only with the Senate, but also with that army—especially when tales got about of his over-fondness for barbarians. Gossip said— and whether it was idle gossip or not, it was believed by soldiers already prejudiced against him—that this fondness extended to dressing himself up in the rude garb of a Scythian warrior and appearing in public in that barbaric guise, making himself an object of contempt to his friends and derision to his foes.

In Britain at this time, the year 382, there was a Spanish soldier holding some high military office (its nature is not clear) called Magnus Clemens Maximus. Fifteen years before, at the time of the Great Invasion, this officer had served under the great general, Theodosius, so that by now, especially as he had a grown son, he must have been at least forty years old. It is difficult to assess the character of this man, for the testimonies of his friends and his detractors conflict violently; but he seems to have been a good soldier, courageous, just, and when circumstances demanded it, lenient; possibly he had other virtues which with these made him very popular with the army of Britain.

In the year 382 he led a revolt of the army of Britain against the emperor. One account says that the soldiery invested him with the purple against his will; another, that he felt resentment against Gratian because he had not received the promotion which he considered his due, and so of his own accord headed the revolt in an attempt to make himself supreme in the West; an action not unprecedented. Whichever account is true, the fact remains that he was proclaimed Augustus by the army of Britain. Thereupon, taking the best of the troops in the diocese with him, and apparently denuding Hadrian's Wall of the bulk of its garrisons in doing so, he crossed to Gaul to substantiate his claim and meet the inevitable conflict with Gratian.

Thus once again, as in the days of Albinus long before, the ambition of a Roman general left Britain at the mercy of its foes. Most authorities nowadays agree that Hadrian's Wall was abandoned soon after 382, and that this represents

the first step in the ruin of the diocese. Almost certainly
Maximus intended replacing the troops he had withdrawn
from the island when his ambitions had been satisfied. In
the event they never were replaced. Maximus won several
initial victories in Gaul—where Gratian was murdered by
one of his own officers who thought to curry favour with
the usurper, whom he considered the winning horse, and
Spain having submitted to him without a fight, Maximus
speedily became master of the western Praefecture of the
Gauls: that is, Britain, Gaul, Spain and Tingitania
(Morocco).

Gratian's successor in Italy was his very young and weak
brother, Valentinian II. The ministers of this puppet
emperor, seeing no other course possible, patched up a peace
with Maximus, which kept him at bay for a couple of years.
No one, however, supposed that this situation would remain
long unchanged. Nor did it. In the third year Maximus
decided to cross the Alps into Italy and be rid of Valentinian
II. Immediately, leaving the usurper's advance unopposed,
Valentinian fled in panic to Constantinople to implore help
from the emperor of the East.

This was now Theodosius the Younger—or 'the Great',
as he is usually called—son of that saviour of Britain in 369
who had been the victim of the jealousy of Valens, the
Eastern emperor of that time. Valens himself had been
killed, shortly after the elder Theodosius's execution, at the
catastrophic battle of Adrianople, when, defeated by the
Goths, 40,000 Romans are said to have lost their lives; and
Gratian had chosen the younger Theodosius, then living
quietly in retirement on his Spanish estates, to succeed to the
throne of the East. At the time of the young Valentinian's
panic-stricken flight to him Theodosius had his hands full
with other wars in the East. So since Maximus was now
supreme in Britain, Gaul, Spain and Tingitania and
Theodosius saw no immediate prospect of dislodging him,
he felt there was nothing he could do but accept the situation.
He acknowledged Maximus as ruler of the Praefecture of the
Gauls, but required him to leave the young Valentinian in
possession of the Praefecture of Italy. Whether Theodosius,
considering the strength of Maximus's ambitions and his hold

over his army, thought this arrangement would be permanent, is doubtful. It did, in fact, last three years. But in 387 Maximus invaded Italy. Immediately the government of Valentinian II collapsed, and once more the boy emperor fled to Theodosius, leaving Maximus emperor of all the West.

This, of course, brought Maximus to a confrontation with Theodosius. The end of his short glory came in 388. In that year he was defeated and captured, and executed near Aquileia, in the region where Venice was later to stand, at the head of the Adriatic Sea.

For so brief a glory, lasting six years, Maximus had sacrificed the safety of Britain. Evidence is conflicting as to the exact date when the Picts on the north, the Irish on the west, and the Saxons on the east, seeing the land almost bereft of garrisons, recommenced with virtual impunity their devastating raids; but all agree that by the time of Magnus Maximus's death these attacks were once again in full swing. The Irish onslaught was especially virulent. It fell with greatest fury upon Wales, and was led by the famous Niall of the Nine Hostages, High King of Ireland. The Irish made no immediate settlements, but they were the authors of a vast amount of ruin. They harried the open country-side, burnt villa after villa as far as the estuary of the Severn, and wherever they could put an end to civilized life. It was in one of these raids that the son of a British decurion was captured and carried off as a slave-boy to Ireland. His name was Patricius. All Ireland was to know him later as St. Patrick.

The country-dwellers were at the mercy of the invaders. Only those escaped who could shut themselves up behind town-walls, for the marauders, like most barbarians, did not attempt sieges. Perhaps now and then a few cavalry units of the remnants of the army of Britain might accost these plunderers and drive them back to their ships; but while the Picts were crashing through Hadrian's deserted Wall and the Saxon pirates were looting and destroying along the eastern coasts how could the depleted army deal with the situation? Well might the poet Claudian make Britannia cry, 'I was perishing at the hands of the neighbouring peoples! For the Scotti brought the whole of Ireland against me, and the sea creamed white beneath the accursed beat of their oars! . . . But now', Claudian makes Britannia conclude, 'I tremble no more because of the Picts. No longer do I look out along the line of my shore, fearing with every change of wind to see the Saxons drawing near. To Stilicho I owe it: he has defended me.'

The poem in which the court poet and former panegyrist of Theodosius, Claudian, makes Britannia utter these words was composed in praise of Flavius Stilicho. This famous general, a comrade-in-arms of the younger Theodosius, whose niece he had married, was, like practically all the Roman generals from now onwards, of barbarian extraction —a Vandal, in fact; for not only were Rome's armies now composed largely of barbarian mercenaries, but their commanders had barbarian forebears also, even if they were sufficiently romanized themselves to consider themselves Romans. When Theodosius died in 395 he left Stilicho as regent in charge of his two young and inefficient sons, Honorius, a boy of eleven being on his father's death emperor of the West, and Arcadius, aged seventeen, emperor of the East. About Stilicho's character, as about Magnus Maximus's, there are conflicting reports; but it seems unquestionable that his loyalty to the family of Theodosius was sincere, and that he fought valiantly to preserve the Empire of his old comrade-in-arms for his undeserving, weak and vacillating sons. Claudian speaks, probably without exaggeration, of the panic which fell upon the citizens of Milan when the warrior hordes of Alaric the Goth drew near, and of their joyful relief when they saw afar the approach of the imperial army with Stilicho's 'famous white head' in the van.

Whether that 'famous white head' was ever seen in Britain is unknown—it may or may not have been. But after a succession of disastrous years when Britain's woes seem to have been unregarded by those in authority Stilicho turned his attention to the diocese.

Stilicho's reorganization of the defences of Britain possibly took place about the year 397. Very likely he did not personally visit Britain—at least, Claudian does not say so— he is more likely to have given instructions to his deputies, who then crossed to Britain and carried out his commands. No details of this reorganization are mentioned, but we may take it that it included the elaboration and strengthening of already existing defence-works, especially on the Yorkshire coast, where, as we have seen, signal-stations had already been built by the elder Theodosius after the Great Invasion. Some authorities believe that it was Stilicho who actually had these signal-stations built; but it is more likely that what Stilicho's lieutenants did was to transform these outlook posts into redoubts. At the same time the walls of some cities in the south-east—first and foremost London—were strengthened by bastions capable of supporting the heavy *ballistae*, the artillery of the time.

These were defensive measures. 'He *defended* me', says Claudian. There is no suggestion of considering attack as the best form of defence. The idea was to drive off the eastern foe—the Saxon—after he had come; not to stop him from coming. Such aggressive tactics were no longer possible—and not only in Britain. Throughout the Empire there were not troops enough any longer adequately to maintain its integrity; the Roman Empire was now beset by hostile barbarians on every frontier.

Stilicho thus took steps to defend the eastern parts of Britain against the Saxons. The Wall area must have been written off as a dead loss, since it was never garrisoned again. But what of the west—the area that had been suffering the scourge of the Irish raids? We know that by this time the Second Legion had been withdrawn from Isca to strengthen the defences of the Saxon Shore Fort at Rutupiae; we know too that the Twentieth Legion, formerly at Deva, had disappeared from the muster roll; the remnants of the Sixth were guarding the Yorkshire coast. What did Stilicho do, then, to defend Wales against the Irish?

It seems that he resorted to an old Roman practice of settling friendly tribes who dwelt outside the frontiers in those areas inside them liable to the attacks of foes. Such tribes would be bound by treaty (*foedus*) to Rome, and were therefore known as *Foederati*; many were already established in several parts of the Empire. North of Hadrian's Wall were the Votadini, for many years friendly to Rome.

Apparently Stilicho made *foederati* of them, and encouraged them, under their romanized prince Cunedda, to come south-westwards into Wales.   Welsh legend speaks of this Cunedda coming 'with his eight sons to Gwynedd' (north-west Wales and Anglesey), where he 'drove out the Irish from those parts and founded a local dynasty'.   Much later the Welsh poet Taliesin makes Cunedda (modern Kenneth) a hero of Cymric Wales and describes his 'golden belt' of authority and his escort of cavalry.   It is clear, therefore, that this part of the diocese, which the Romans no longer had the means to defend, was defending itself under native princes with official approval against the Irish foe.

Thus Stilicho did what he could to re-establish the defences of Britain during the closing years of the fourth century, and to reassert Roman authority there.   But in 402 the Visigoths led by Alaric began their attacks upon Italy itself.   For the first time the barbarians, watching the Empire's growing weakness and seizing their opportunity, showed their intention of striking even at Rome, the very heart of the West. To confront Alaric with some hope of success Stilicho was obliged to draw away out of Britain one of the two remaining legions—probably the Sixth Victrix—weakening once more the very defences he had lately strengthened.

He defeated Alaric at the battle of Pollentia.   Almost immediately afterwards there penetrated even further into Italy another barbarian invasion led by the Goth Radagaisus.   Stilicho could not spare the British legion he had withdrawn, and it was not sent back to the island.   In 405 Radagaisus was in his turn defeated and killed.   But then a third wave of the encroaching sea mounted high and swept all before it.   On the last night of the old year, 406, a confederacy of Suevi, Vandals, Alani and Burgundians in one vast horde crossed the frozen Rhine and swarmed into Gaul.   They showed an ability to take walled cities which was unusual among barbarians.   Cutting down the Frankish *foederati*, the frontier-guard of the lower Rhine who made a vain attempt to repulse them, and surging onwards, they stormed and sacked Treveri, the headquarters of the praetorian prefect of Gaul, and as the Roman defence-line crumpled up, Arras, Amiens, Paris, Orleans and Tours fell to them. 'All France smoked like a funeral-pyre', says St. Orientius.

The suffering of the Gauls now equalled those of recent years among the Britons, as the Alemanni joined the invaders. Sweeping westwards and southwards the barbarian hordes at last reached Tolosa (Toulouse) far in the south, where they were at length repulsed by the Roman garrison.

But now a broad belt of devastation and barbarian occupation lay spread right across Gaul, cutting the lines of communication between Rome and Britain; the Rhine frontier, established for four hundred years, had been broken, and was never to be restored again. The fall of the Western Empire seemed imminent.

XVI · 'NOW FADES THE GLIMMERING LANDSCAPE ON THE SIGHT'

This was the moment chosen by the army of Britain to set up another usurper. Actually it set up three, one after the other, but its first and second choices were speedily murdered, and only the third—bearing the illustrious name of Constantine, though there was nothing else very illustrious about him—survived his elevation for four years. The cause of this mutiny against established authority was despair at the perilous straits in which the Britons found themselves, encompassed as they were by enemies, and resentment against Stilicho for doing nothing to help them. For to Britain Stilicho's eyes seemed now always directed eastwards, and engaged in his Gothic war he was no longer paying any attention to the woes of Britain. So the Britons decided to raise up a leader of their own, and after choosing badly twice they saluted Constantine, a Briton, as their emperor to rule over them and put matters right. But when they made this decision the Britons had no more thought than they had had in the days of Magnus Maximus of breaking away from the Roman Empire; such an idea would have been inconceivable to them.

Constantine is described as a 'common soldier of low origin', but he was evidently more capable than the two murdered leaders who had preceded him, though his capabilities were misdirected. Instead of stopping in Britain and using what talents he had in organizing and strengthening the defences of the diocese, and guarding the land against the enemies pressing in upon it, he followed the example set by Magnus Maximus a quarter of a century before. He appointed a *vicarius*, or governor, to direct the civil administration, and then, taking probably the Second Legion and some of the best of the auxiliaries, leaving behind only a part as an inadequate garrison, in the year 407 he crossed, as Maximus had done, to Gaul, and called upon the troops there to join him. Here at last, it seemed to the distraught Gauls, was a champion close at hand to drive the barbarians away, a thing which Stilicho had failed to do; and so such of the army of the Gauls as was left from the devastation wrought by the barbarian flood of 406–7 joined Constantine, and proclaimed him emperor.

But he was a complete disappointment to Britons and Gauls alike. He did nothing to expel the Vandals and Burgundians from Gaul; his main idea seemed to be securing the Rhine frontier, which had been shattered by that midwinter crossing on New Year's Eve and strengthening his own position by adding Spain to the lands over which he held sway. By the year 410 his attempts to hold a Rhine frontier had broken down, Alaric was marching on Rome, and Stilicho, the best general of the time, and the only real defender of the Western Empire, had fallen a victim to the jealousy of his enemies and been executed. A year later Constantine, besieged in Arles in southern Gaul, was captured, and in his turn executed in Ravenna. What remained of his army—the troops of which he had denuded Britain just over three years before—was never sent back to the diocese; we have no idea what became of the Second Legion.

But a year before Constantine's downfall and death a crisis had occurred in the diocese. The fateful year 410, though it does not mark the end of Roman Britain, draws a distinct line of cleavage across its history.

Britain had expected much from Constantine, and when he achieved nothing, while the raids of the Saxons increased upon the eastern coasts, now more inadequately defended than ever before, the indignant provincials angrily expelled the *vicarius* and the administrative officers whom Constantine had left behind, and then sent messages to Honorius to despatch to them officers to command the troops they still had left and carry on the work of civil administration. The message brought forth from Honorius, unable to accede to their requests, his famous rescript of 410, in which he instructed the British tribal authorities to carry on the work of government themselves till he could send them his own nominees, and meanwhile to look to their own defence.

For a disaster had befallen Honorius and Italy which had

shaken the whole Western world. Alaric and his Visigoths had overrun Italy, and invested Rome. One of the gates of the city had been opened by treachery, and the hordes of Alaric had broken in and for three days had slaughtered, outraged and plundered. They looted the jewels and silks of the senators and laid their hands upon all the treasures of luxurious living; they took prisoners and either held them to ransom or enslaved them. Those who could escape fled in broken array to Africa or the East, crying out that 'eternal Rome, mother and light of the world, had been sacked by barbarians'.

Though for many years Rome had no longer been the seat of government of the Western Empire there was a prestige about her very name throughout the whole world—even the barbarian world. Even the Christian Tertullian, an enemy of everything pagan, had called her 'sacrosanct'; to another Christian, Lactantius, she was, under God, the sole bulwark of society; beyond her lay darkness and chaos. Rome was something that had always been, must always be, unshaken and unshakable; to men's minds it was unthinkable that she should ever be overthrown. In fact, the *Fortuna Urbis*, the mystical divinity which was Rome, had affected men's minds so powerfully through all the long centuries of her reign, that its influence was to last on into the Middle Ages. It has been truly said that Rome was the mightiest ghost that ever troubled the affairs of living men; 'The Roman legend', says Helen Waddell, 'was to be the creative inspiration of Europe.' Only one other city has ever fallen with such resounding repercussions, and that was Constantinople, a thousand and fifty years after, the eastern remnant of the once mighty Roman Empire which had formerly embraced almost the whole known world.

It is certain that neither Honorius nor the Britons intended or dreamt that this independence of action commanded by the emperor should be permanent. The Britons obeyed his instructions, took up arms on their own account and governed themselves as best they might simply because at the time there had seemed nothing else to be done. Honorius had sent his rescript because at the moment of its despatch the world had fallen about his ears and he had no help of any kind to send to Rome's most northerly province. No doubt both parties were blind to the fact that the temporal power of Rome in the West was waning, never to wax again. In the event, as we know, Rome's long day, as far as the Western Empire was concerned, was declining to its sunset, and although the twilight lingered till 476 when the last ineffective emperor of the West, the boy Romulus Augustulus —so ironically named—was deposed and pensioned off by the barbarian leader Odovacar, its sun had set long before.

So there was never any conscious or deliberate severance of Britain from the Roman Empire. For a long while, indeed, Britain still expected that a resurrected Roman power would come to her aid and that she would be once more governed by the central authority. There are some historians at the present time who think that for a brief period there actually was a reoccupation of the province by Rome, and that from about 417 to 429 a Roman *vicarius* did head the civil administration and a Roman field army did deal for a little while with Britain's barbarian enemies; but this it is impossible either to prove or disprove. Certain it is, however, that far into the fifth century the Britons still considered themselves Roman citizens, still fondly dreamt that the legions would return, and that the Roman way of life, Roman thought and civilization and government would come again, and that the world would be as it had been before.

We are entering now upon dark and obscure ways. The lengthening shadows of approaching night crowd one upon the other, shutting out the light of day. We walk, as it were, lost in a tangled wood, where only now and then the gleam of a lantern shoots a ray to illumine the darkness, then vanishes again, leaving us to grope more blindly even than before. For we are drawing near the period known to historians of Britain as 'The Lost Centuries'—those barely recorded years in which Rome's most northerly province was changed, we cannot at present trace by what steps, into the heptarchy of Anglo-Saxon England.

It would appear, from the few flashes of lantern-light that are vouchsafed us, that in the larger towns of Britain cantonal government as it had been exercised under the Romans continued, for a few decades, to exist. We know, therefore, that the Britons did not immediately succumb to the invaders, but put up a stiff fight against them now they were left to their own resources. In the more remote districts men fell back again, it would seem, upon the strength of the old tribal chieftainships which had existed before the Romans had come, and in the more mountainous districts were able to adopt guerrilla tactics to keep the invaders at bay, although now along Hadrian's Wall only the flotsam and jetsam of abandoned forts and ghosts of the imperial Roman frontier defence that had crumbled away before men's eyes remained on this extremity of Rome's once invincible Empire. One clear and well authenticated incident, which throws light upon conditions nearly twenty years after Honorius's rescript we do hear of in Constantius's *Life of St. Germanus*, the bishop of Auxerre, written in the last quarter of the fifth century.

Germanus, Constantius tells us, first came to Britain with his friend Lupus, bishop of Troyes, in 429, to preach against a heresy within the Christian Church of Britain about Free Will, first started by a Briton called Pelagius. (The fact that Britons at this date could be concerned with such theological questions and heretical disputes surely argues against any wholesale swamping of the population by barbarian hordes as yet.) Moreover the 'Life' tells us that the supporters of the heresy, all *wealthy magnates arrayed in splendid apparel*, came to meet Germanus, who preached against the heresy at a synod held at Verulamium, where the bishops did reverence to the shrine of St. Alban. This does not sound as if all the cities—if any—of the south-east had been laid waste by Saxons by 429, nor all the Britons reduced to poverty and rags, although at that very time the Picts and the Saxons were 'undertaking war against the Britons with conjoined forces, the one from the land, the other from the sea'. Picts and Saxons only, it seems; the Irish (or Scotti) are not mentioned. It may perhaps be assumed that the descendants of Cunedda had finally driven them from Wales and the western coasts; and as Christianity was soon to be brought to Ireland by St. Patrick, returning on his divine mission long after he had escaped from slavery in Ireland, their wild spirits were presently to be tamed, and when they came again it was not to bring war, but the peace of the Christian faith.

The story told in the *Life of St. Germanus* goes on to say that the Britons were much concerned by the violence of this attack of Picts and Saxons, and asked Germanus to help them. This may sound odd, until we remember that in his youth Germanus had been a great man of war, and had held high military command with distinction. He took the situation in hand most effectively. He gathered together all the fighting forces still available, and instructed them what to do. Then when he, with the army so mustered, had come a little to the north of Verulamium the bishop chose a battlefield to the greatest advantage for the army of Britain. It was a narrow, flat valley bounded by very high hills (this does not sound like 'a little to the north of Verulamium'—the fight must have taken place much farther north or west); and as the hills lay folded one behind the other he hid many of the army here and there on either side in the folds. So as the enemy came down the valley some of the Britons lay in ambush on their flanks; the rest remained in front, in view of the advancing foe. Then, instructed by Germanus, they waited for his signal; and when the Picts and Saxons had advanced far enough, making for those they could see in front of them, not suspecting any ambush, Germanus gave the signal. Straightway the Britons visible to the enemy in front shouted the war-cry they had been bidden to shout: *Alleluia!* and as the enemy stood surprised the shout was taken up not only by those in ambush but by the hills themselves, which echoed and re-echoed it, so that the foe imagined their antagonists to be fifty times as many as they really were. Surrounded and ambushed, and as they believed, outnumbered, the Picts and Saxons offered no resistance, but flung their encumbering shields and spears away and fled back down the valley. The Britons pursued them, some rushing after them along the valley, the rest pouring down from every fold of the hills. Most of the enemy were cut down; and some, while trying to cross the river which lay across their flight, mistook the ford and were drowned.

This story of the 'Alleluia Victory' sheds a clear, if

M

short-lived light upon the condition of Britain in the year 429. It shows that though the towns may have been decaying they nevertheless survived; that civil government was still functioning, that there was still some wealth and prosperity to bring forth citizens 'arrayed in splendid apparel', that men still had opportunity and inclination to consider spiritual things, and above all that they not only had the will to defend themselves but when they were properly led could drive off the enemy very effectively.

But when Germanus came a second time to Britain on a similar mission, eighteen years later, the situation had degenerated considerably. It had been in the preceding year, 446, according to the *Liber Querulus* of the west-British monk Gildas (who wrote 130 years after the event, about 545) that the Britons had sent a letter which he calls, in his usual emotional fashion, *The Groans of the Britons*, to the Roman general Aëtius, an eminent officer who had lately restored Roman authority in south and central Gaul and had become, in 433, virtual ruler of the West. This letter was a last appeal to Rome for help in dire extremity. 'The barbarians', the appeal cried, 'drive us to the sea, the sea throws us back on the barbarians; we have only the choice between the two methods of death—whether we should be massacred or drowned.'

But Aëtius had other things to think about as he wallowed through a succession of wars against Rome's enemies on the Continent. He did not reply to this appeal for help. Perhaps the Britons had thought that Germanus might succour them again when he appeared a second time in the land to refute heresy once more; but we hear of nothing that he did on this occasion to mitigate the Britons' troubles, and he died in Gaul in the following year.

It was probably after this last vain appeal to Aëtius that the Britons finally abandoned all hope of ever becoming part of the Roman Empire again, of ever being considered Roman citizens as in the days of old, speaking the language of Rome and living in accordance with her civilized laws and ways. It was from about 446 onwards that life was falling back into greater and greater barbarism as the culture of Rome was being forgotten.

The story now grows more than ever confused, conflicting and uncertain. We have little to guide us besides the tirades of the highly emotional monk Gildas, who did not write (a hundred years after the event, anyway) to enlighten future ages on the history of the fifth century, but to castigate the sins of certain contemporary kings, and whose jeremiads are overwrought, exaggeratedly rhetorical, and historically speaking unreliable. According to his account there flourished about the middle of the fifth century a chieftain— '*superbus tyrannus*' Gildas calls him; he wrote, of course, in Latin—who reigned in the manner of a king in South Wales, and had some sort of power over other areas of Britain. Gildas gives no names, but we learn his name from another source (assuming that this source is dealing with the same individual), the even more historically unreliable *Historia Brittonum*, a farago of wild legends and incredible miracles compiled anonymously about 685 and added to and redacted in the ninth century by Nennius.   It was Vortigern.

Vortigern, when the Pictish invasions started again, seems to have followed a Roman practice which we have mentioned before, that of hiring mercenaries and retaining them as *foederati* in the land to fight the foes they had not themselves the resources to confront unaided.   The leader of these particular mercenaries (again, Gildas does not give his name; to him he is merely one of the 'wolves brought into the sheepcote') was, if we may trust the *Historia Brittonum*, Hengist, with his brother Horsa.   Hengist did what was required of him, and then, because adequate payment was not forthcoming, he with his 'dogs of mercenaries' broke out of the lands that had been granted them, and together with all their friends and relations who had crossed the sea to aid and abet them, swept over the whole of southern Britain, massacring, driving out or enslaving the Roman provincials.

Gildas now gets into his stride.   'The conflagration that they started in the east', he writes, 'was spread from sea to sea; it blazed across every city and region, nor did it stay its burning course until, after devastating almost the whole surface of the island, its ruddy tongues licked the Western Ocean [the Bristol Channel].   Every colony is levelled to the ground by the stroke of the battering-ram, the inhabitants are slaughtered along with the guardians of their churches, priests and people alike, while the sword gleamed on every side and the flames crackled around. The tops of towers are torn from their lofty hinges, the stones of high walls . . . there was no grave for the dead unless they were buried under the wretched ruins of their homes. Of the miserable remnant some flee to the hills only to be captured and slain in heaps. Some, constrained by famine, come in and surrender themselves to be slaves to the enemy if only their lives might be spared; others, wailing bitterly, passed overseas.'

Shorn of its hysteria, this is probably a fairly truthful picture of the disastrous sequel to the invitation to Hengist and Horsa to settle their war-bands in Britain; except that the 'conflagration' was very likely not as swift and sudden as Gildas makes it out to be, but ate its way inexorably but more slowly across the land. It may even be that the event mentioned under the year 490 by the Anglo-Saxon Chronicle (compiled at least four centuries later, and therefore, for this period, even more historically unreliable than Gildas) may, although forty years after the generally accepted date of Hengist's coming, belong to this era of devastation. 'This year', the Chronicle says, 'Aella and Cissa besieged the city of Andred [that is, the Saxon Shore fort of Anderida, modern Pevensey] and slew all that were therein, nor was one Briton left there afterwards.' A pathetic reflection upon the state of Britain long after the Romans had abandoned it to shift for itself; for 'all that were therein' would probably not be soldiers, but desperate refugees, thinking to find some safety behind the massive Roman walls of the fort. Excavation at Pevensey has found no signs of this massacre; but it is the kind of thing that might well have happened as the fifth century was drawing to its close.

The lost centuries are growing steadily more irrecoverable. The shadows enveloping them are like ghosts flitting inconsequently across the night. Gildas mentions by name an evanescent figure, Ambrosius Aurelianus, who, he states, after the onrush of Hengist and his barbarian hordes, rallied a British remnant still resisting the invader among the woods, mountains and crags by the sea. The *Historia Brittonum* tells

of a *dux bellorum* named Arthur.   Both are credited with a
resounding victory over the Saxons at Mount Badon—
wherever that may have been.   Were they one and the same
person understandably confused in folk memory?   Or is
Ambrosius Aurelianus alone historical, and Arthur nothing
but a myth?   That Ambrosius Aurelianus existed there is
no good reason to doubt, nor that when the wave of invasion
had swept across part of Britain, however long that may have
taken, he as military leader rallied the Britons and
temporarily checked it; but we are not so certain that Arthur
was a real person, and not rather an invention of later times,
a 'hero of romance', who has been wrongly credited with
the valiant deeds of the real Ambrosius.

But more and more authorities these days tend to believe
that Arthur was a real person, who perhaps followed after
Ambrosius Aurelianus, and that he fought a rearguard
action in a last desperate attempt to save what was left of
Roman civilization in Britain.   Not the supreme high king
of the twelfth-century Geoffrey of Monmouth, still less the
very perfect knight of the Victorian Tennyson; but a military
chief of the Roman pattern, a hard-pressed Romano-Briton
of good family who still held memories of the Roman Britain
that had been, leading a tough war-band against a persistent
enemy; the 'last of the Romans' in the darkening twilight
of a Britain fast forgetting Roman days and Roman ways.

We can go no farther.   The truth shatters into fragments
like brittle glass in our hands.   We stand among the tumbled
stones of Hadrian's Wall, Rome's one-time northernmost
frontier of Empire, and meditate upon that melancholy
'*Sic transit gloria mundi*'—thus passes the glory of the world—
and as we so meditate, all we have left is the nostalgic
legend told by the men of old, that somewhere beneath
Sewingshields Crags on Hadrian's Wall Arthur still sleeps,
to awaken again to lead his British hosts into battle against
her foes when Britain in dire peril once more shall again
have need of him.

BOOKS FOR FURTHER READING

Blair, P. Hunter: *Roman Britain and Early England*, Nelson, 1963.
Burn, A. R.: *Agricola and Roman Britain*, English Universities Press, 1953.
Collingwood, Bruce J. (ed. I. A. Richmond): *The Roman Wall*, Andrew Reid, 1951.
Collingwood and Myres: *Roman Britain and the English Settlements: Oxford History of England*, Oxford University Press, 1945.
Collingwood, R. G.: *Roman Britain*, Clarendon Press, 1953.
Forestier, Amédée: *The Roman Soldier* (with special reference to Britain—largely a picture book), A. and C. Black, 1928.
Gibbon, Edward: *Decline and Fall of the Roman Empire*, 6 vols., Dent, 1936–8.
— Abridged version in one vol. *The Great Histories Series*, ed. Hugh Trevor-Roper, New English Library, 1966.
Home, Gordon: *Roman London*, Eyre and Spottiswoode, 1948.
Lewis, M. J. T.: *Temples in Roman Britain*, Cambridge University Press, 1967.
Liversidge, Joan: *Furniture in Roman Britain*, Tiranti, 1955.
Meates, Col. G. W.: *Lullingstone Roman Villa*, Heinemann, 1955.
Oman, Sir Charles: *England before the Norman Conquest*, Books I and II, Methuen, 1938.
Previté-Orton, C. W.: *The Shorter Cambridge Mediaeval History*, Books I and II (from Constantine to the break-up of the Roman Empire in the West), Cambridge University Press, 1952.
Richmond, Ian A.: *Roman Britain*, Penguin, 1955.
— *Roman Britain and Roman Military Antiquities*, Proceedings of the British Academy, O.U.P., 1955.
Rivet, A. L. F.: *Town and Country in Roman Britain*, Hutchinson, 1958.
Tacitus, Publius Cornelius: *Agricola et Germania* (Latin Text), Pitt Press, C.U.P.
— *Agricola on Britain and Germany* (translation by H. Mattingly), Penguin Books, 1951.
Toynbee, Jocelyn: *Art in Roman Britain*, Phaidon, 1962.
Wheeler, Sir Mortimer: *Report on the Excavations at Lydney Park, Gloucestershire*, Oxford, 1952.
— *Verulamium: A Belgic and Two Roman Towns* (excavators' report), Oxford, 1936.
Map of Roman Britain (Third Edition) Ordnance Survey, 1956.

WHERE TO SEE COLLECTIONS OF OBJECTS FROM ROMAN BRITAIN

The British Museum, Bloomsbury, London, W.C.

The Guildhall Museum, 55 Bassishaw High Walk, London, E.C.2. (*Items from the City including those from the Walbrook (Mithraic Temple) Site.*)

The National Museum of Wales, Cardiff.

Museum of Roman Antiquities, The Hospitium, Philosophical Society's Grounds, York.

The Colchester and Essex Museum, Norman Castle, Colchester.

The Grosvenor Museum, Chester. (*Very fine collection of sculptured tombstones.*)

Blackgate Museum, Newcastle-on-Tyne (*Chiefly items found along Hadrian's Wall.*)

Tullie House Museum, Carlisle.

Roman Baths Museum, Bath. (*Items of local provenance.*)

Newport Museum, Monmouthshire. (*The 'Caerwent' Room—mostly from Caerwent and Caerleon.*)

The London Museum, Kensington Palace. (*Objects found in London only.*)

Chesters Museum, Cilurnum, Chollerford. (*Objects found in or near the fort of Cilurnum, Hadrian's Wall. Very extensive array of Roman altars.*)

Corinium Museum, Cirencester. (*Interesting exhibits, attractively arranged, but unfortunately most are undated.*)

The City and County Museum, Lincoln. (*Local finds.*)

This list is not exhaustive. Only museums containing extensive or outstanding collections have been included. Many Roman villas open to the public have their own museums of site finds.

INDEX